# It Doesr You're Selling

## Six Bulletproof Moves For Getting More Clients, Massive Income, and a Customer Base That Believes In You

### Andrew "Superstar" Kaplan

Published by Awesome Marvelous, Inc. – New York

# Table of Contents:

# FREE Bonus Resources -- GO HERE FIRST

The book you now hold in your hands is going to reveal a high-level deep-impact playbook for taking your sales and marketing numbers to the next level.

But the rabbit hole can go really deep if you let it. And you want to start boosting your revenue NOW.

So in order to help you take immediate steps to bring in cash flow (rather than wandering off and distracting yourself with something else), I've chosen very specific bonuses for you. They will build right off of each chapter, and they'll allow you to take strong action on what you learn WITHOUT taking long to consume.

These bonus resources are sharp, to the point, and ready to implement right away.

Each one normally comes with a high-price tag, but they're yours for free as a thank you for reading this book and taking action on your success. This is how we win.

I'll describe each bonus a little more at the end of each chapter that it relates to, but you can grab them all up right now by going to:

## www.ItDoesntMatterBook.com

# In this book, you'll learn:

A lot of awesome stuff.

We're going to take your sales and marketing skills on a journey of true dynamic growth through 6 core strategies:

In Chapter 1, you're going to learn what it really takes to position yourself and your product in a truly epic way that will have prospects clamoring for YOUR solution from miles away.

In Chapter 2, you're going to understand how buyers REALLY notice what you have to offer, and why grabbing their attention in very specific ways makes a huge difference in your results.

In Chapter 3, you're going to discover a brand new method of piercing the minds and hearts of your customers through storytelling methods that speak to their actual biology.

In Chapter 4, you're going to learn the art of the "value pile" and how it takes regular boring stand-alone products and turns them into offers that just can't be ignored.

In Chapter 5, you're going to understand how to put yourself and your product directly in front of a market that's primed to buy whatever you're selling.

In Chapter 6, you're going to discover the bulletproof mindset needed for having a product or service you that can sell at any time and at any price.

# ABOUT THE AUTHOR
## (And why you should care)

It takes a certain mindset to fund a Kickstarter campaign in 30 hours (with a list of less than 100 people), write and publish a book in only 24 hours, AND beat out over 800 applicants for a job with WWE.

More importantly, it takes a very strategic approach. Especially when you're going to advise others on taking their business results to the next level as well.

But Andrew Kaplan's entrepreneurial journey wasn't always exactly a walk in the park.

In fact, when Andrew began his first company straight out of school, he had one strategy: See what's already working, and copy as close as you can. Little did he know how much failure that would lead to.

Because if you want to throw a football like Tom Brady, it's not enough to study how his arm moves. You also need to learn his footwork, communicate with your receivers, and understand the team's entire offense.

In other words, Andrew was never going to succeed by doing what everyone else did ...until he figured out WHY those things worked in the first place.

But now, after over ten years of doing this in the real world, where it counts, Andrew gets it. And his clients are the ones throwing touchdowns.

Of all the big wins that Andrew attributes to his track record, he considers one of the most important ones his discovery of Direct Response Copywriting.

This is an underground century-old style of selling that Andrew would discover was behind every successful strategy that he ever modeled when he was younger. And as soon as he started to work with these concepts and techniques, things really took off.

On his road to success, Andrew cut his teeth in just about every competitive market segment you can find.

By forcing himself to understand the psychology of a buyer in so many different areas, Andrew has uniquely positioned himself to train entrepreneurs and salespeople across countless industries. His clients close more customers, position themselves more powerfully, and refine their marketing and sales strategies way more effectively.

When it came time to publish the book you now hold in your hands, Andrew had himself a branding issue. See, he always wanted to write books that obliterated all confusion around sales and marketing.

Problem was, there was already an Andrew Kaplan out there who established himself as an author.

Not wanting to waste time or money on the Amazon and Google search algorithm problems that would result from having more than one 'Andrew Kaplan' out there, he published under a nickname he had become known on his very first podcast: The Marketing Sales Superstar (since replaced by the ground-breaking "Shatter The Mold").

A name that would be hard to miss: "Superstar" Kaplan.

'Superstar' is the founder and CEO of Awesome Marvelous, Inc., a firm devoted to helping clients through their own sales challenges, putting their messaging and marketing strategy on steroids, and driving their performance and results way further in the process. No needle required.

He's been featured in Men's Health, on Playboy Radio, and on Hot97 in New York City, where he currently resides.

You can learn more (and occasionally even sneak in some free consulting that would normally run you thousands of dollars) by catching him on his "Shatter The Mold" Podcast, where he explores business concepts, marketing strategies, human psychology, and so much more.

For those who don't get to check the show out, this book will offer various free resources that Kaplan assembled just for you, but if you want to pick up even more new tactics and insights right away, you can learn more about his podcast by going to: www.ShatterTheMoldPodcast.com

# INTRODUCTION - The #1 Reason People Will Buy From You ...When All Else Is Equal

The number one reason people will buy from YOU ...when all else is equal.

I bet you'd love to know what that is, right?

We'll get to that, trust me.

Oh, and we'll do it in THIS intro chapter. I'm not about to make you read through the entire rest of the book wondering what it is.

Don't you hate when all those other dickhead authors pull that shit? They offer you some huge earth-shattering secret that's going to change everything for you, but only if you're willing to comb through the next 400 pages to get there.

Probably because those insecure losers need the ego stroke of you frantically pouring through their work, desperately paying attention to every last word.

Well, not in my house, my friend. Not in my fucking house.

No, we're going to clearly state the number one reason people will buy from you when all else is equal. Before you even get to chapter 1. This is actually happening.

But first (because I now kinda see why those dicks enjoy teasing their readers so much), a quick question for you...

Absolute Sales Domination.

That's what you're really looking for here, right?

With all the people I've worked with over the years, and all the different ways they've asked for help, I can only assume your answer is yes.

There's just no way around it. Whether you're building a marketing campaign for your business, selling someone else's product or service, or even coaching others to closing more clients of their own, the goal is always the same:

Sales. Lots and lots of sales. That, or a Powerball lotto win.

But minus the lottery option, sales are what it all comes down to. From that very first call you make ...to that very first door you knock on ...to that very first headline you write -- all you're looking for is for the prospect to pull out that wallet of theirs and say 'yes'.

And if that's the case, I've got good news and bad news.

The bad news is you've been had. Not by me. I'm the one guy who's gonna tell you the truth.

But you've been had. You've been convinced by all the other talking heads, so-called 'gurus', and best-selling authors that selling requires years of study, an endless array of tactics, and a lot of luck.

But it just doesn't work that way.

Sure, that stuff helps if you've already been through it. EVERY little bit helps. But if you've already been through all of it and you still bought this book, it obviously didn't solve your problem for you.

Because it just isn't enough to consume low or mid-level tactics and then hope for high-level results. It just isn't.

So I'm sorry if I'm the first one to tell you this, but you've probably thrown a lot of time and money away on content that's never going to get you over the top.

But this can technically be turned into a good thing.

Because you received something VITAL in that experience that you probably didn't even notice you were getting:

You got to know and feel what it truly means to be a buyer.

You now know what emotional strings were pulled to get you to take your wallet out and spend your hard-earned cash.

You now know what it's like to hope against hope that "this will finally be the key to turning it all around and making big money."

And you can use that insight to sell more of whatever you're offering to others. And we'll get there.

But that's not even the good news.
No, the good news is way better than that.

The good news can be summed up in three possibly grammatically-incorrect words:

## "SALES IS EASY."

That's what my new friend Amir told me 3 years ago in Cancun. There we were at what I can only describe as an entrepreneurial retreat. Hundreds of like-minded business owners. All looking to turn themselves into millionaires (or for the ones who had already made it there, multi-millionaires).

And there was Amir, a stiff drink in each hand, holding court at the bar after the first day's events. With about seven or eight other people leaning in as closely as they could, all Amir could utter between sips of his Long Island Iced Teas was that "sales is easy, bruh. You just have to realize it."

Now the poor guy was a bit too tipsy to articulate it very well, but he was actually on to something. And as he slurred his way through story after story of his sales conquests, I was starting to spot a pattern in what he was describing.

You see, on the surface, Amir wasn't doing anything special. And that's why it's so hard for a complete stranger to really buy into what he was saying.

But Amir had a special gift. One he might not have even been consciously aware of.

You see, Amir knew how to take simple sales techniques that everyone's heard in their lives, and execute them in a way that was consistent with how the human mind makes decisions. That was the secret to his success.

Now if that sounds complicated, it's not. And if that sounds like an incomplete description, hang on. That's why I wrote this book.

## IT'S ALL ABOUT THE TITLE ...AND SUBTITLE

Let's look at the obvious here and notice that I've titled this book "It Doesn't Matter What You're Selling." But then in the subtitle of the book, I mentioned 6 "moves" that you'll need to make in order for that statement to be true.

These are more than just 'moves,' by the way. They're keys. And the secret to using them is knowing:

- Which doors to open.
- Where those doors are.
- And, most importantly, HOW to turn the key.

Now again, if this sounds complicated, trust me. It isn't. Or it won't be, at least. Not by the time you're done reading this book. In fact, it's so simple, most people refuse to take action and use these keys properly.

Instead, they half-ass their sales and marketing attempts, quickly get frustrated, quit, start over, and end up repeating the same mistakes all over again. Only this time, they've slightly modified what they're doing. But they still haven't really changed all that much. And on the next go-around, they're tired, jaded, and slower to act.

But it doesn't have to be this way for you.

Why?

Because "sales is easy."

## THERE'S LIGHT AT THE END OF THE TUNNEL

# IT DOESN'T MATTER WHAT YOU'RE SELLING

People want to buy things that will help them. All they need is someone who can provide them with clarity, understands their natural human fear, and can help them get past it.

So with that in mind, before we get into the really high-impact chapters, why don't we drop some immediate value on you and start off with three important "secrets" right away.

I hesitate to call them secrets because I think they're pretty obvious. But for some reason that I still haven't figured out, people seem to have a lot of trouble accepting them. And it's keeping their leads colder than a polar bear's nuts.

Anyway, here they are:

"Secret" #1:
When it comes to selling... all you
need is the right framework.

The human mind receives and accepts information in very specific (and very predictable) ways.

And this is nothing new.

In fact, have you ever considered that drawings on caveman walls might be offering a huge clue on how to access the psyche of today's customer?

These drawings are stories, which we'll devote a chapter to later on. And -- spoiler alert -- some of the best sales pros in the world use stories without even knowing how effective they are. They chalk it up to 'luck' without realizing that anyone else can do exactly what they're doing with only about a day's worth of sales training from me.

If you have any doubt about about what I'm saying here, stop and think about it for a moment. We've got literally hundreds of thousands of years of human psychology genetically coded into us at birth.

That fight vs. flight response still lives inside of us, along with all the other programming designed for keeping us alive long enough to mate with something sexy and keep the species going for a little while longer.

That's why techniques that were used 100 years ago still work today. It's all rooted in how we process information and make decisions. The sooner you recognize this, the more successful you'll be.

So when I say that it's the framework that matters, what I'm telling you is that there are ways of presenting what you're offering that are more effective than you could ever imagine.

I've actually taken consultation call recordings that I did with a plumber and shared them with a software sales rep.

# IT DOESN'T MATTER WHAT YOU'RE SELLING

The plumber gave me the okay to do this, of course. And it's a good thing he did. Because the software rep listened to the calls, applied the same strategies, and starting pulling in some major bank. Proper sales techniques really are that universal.

Obviously there are certain specific things you need to consider for your own individual situation. And both the plumber and software rep each got more special and specific attention. But the beauty of that is that once you understand the common principles that drive sales success for everyone, all those deeper specifics for your particular situation will work themselves out way more easily.

It's all about the way you present your offer. It's all about the framework. And that's what this book is going to provide you with. You'll get an insider look at all the key moves in that framework. You'll understand what order to put them in. You'll execute on the strategy. You'll win. And all your hopes and dreams will come true.

Okay, scratch that last part out. For all I know, your hopes and dreams are to straddle a mechanical bull wearing a pink tutu on one of those Australian talent shows, with each of the judges screaming "touchdown!" and "good on you, mate!" -- all while you set the world record for: "Time Spent a Mechanical Bull Wearing a Pink Dress with Judges Screaming."

So yeah... let's just stop at the previous promise instead: You'll win.

And really, isn't that what you're here for? A big win? Well, sit tight. Because it's coming.

Anyway… moving on.

"Secret" #2:
A confused mind always says 'no'.

Part of the reason that entrepreneurs and salespeople have so much difficulty closing sales is that they don't understand the mindset of their customer.

There are ways to simplify what you're selling that make customers way more receptive to your offer.

Many of the people I've worked with have been SO excited by everything their product offers, that they wanted to shove all the info down their prospect's throat.

And I can't really be mad at them for this. They're excited about what they're selling, after all.

And that's a very good sign. But the animal part of the brain (that was there long before the emotional part, and even longer before the reasoning part) needs to feel safe in order for the message to get through.

What you'll learn in this book will help you format your message so that even if you have a lot to offer with your product or service, the prospect won't feel too overwhelmed by what you have to say. And they'll be receptive to the idea that you can deliver what you promise.

For example, let's say I'm selling a software product that includes email functionality inside of it. And let's say the email functionality includes:

- Email Reply
- Email Forwarding
- Spell Check
- Grammar Check
- Font Types
- Font Colors
- Font Sizes
- Automatic Draft Saving
- Email Sorting Options
- Email Search Features

Well, if this is the case, and I'm telling my prospect about this, I can't just list all of this out to them. It's just too much. Even if ALL of these things are awesome (or if I believe they're all awesome), the prospect won't be able to process everything, and their monkey mind will shut down on you.

But since part of our genetically-programed survival instincts include avoiding conflict, they'll hide the fact that they've tuned you out.

So you'll be on cloud nine talking about how great your software's email section is, and you won't even realize you lost them at 'Email Forwarding.'

But what if instead, you chose the MOST DESIRED feature from the list (which you will find out from asking customers and NOT just assuming that you already know), and described your email functionality like this:

"EVERYTHING you would expect from a standard email account, including (insert most desired feature here)!"

Pay close attention to what I did just there.  Because if you haven't been doing it already, you really should be able to describe your product or service in only one or two sentences.

When you can do that, you'll know that you've made it easy enough for the prospect's monkey mind to process.  And you'll know that they'll now be paying attention to you instead of silently saying 'no' to themselves right away.

If that seems too basic, you probably need to hear our third secret...

"Secret" #3:
Your sales and marketing methods
DON'T need to be original.

# IT DOESN'T MATTER WHAT YOU'RE SELLING

Have you ever seen the movie "Training Day?" Denzel Washington stars as Alonzo, a crooked cop with a nearly flawless talent for influencing everyone around him. He gets them to respond in predictable ways by understanding their psychology and human motivations.

One of Alonzo's go-to lines in the movie is "Do you want to go home or do you want to go to jail?"

It's a great line when you think about it. Here's this crooked cop who really can't be reasoned with, and he's giving you a choice between two options that he's already decided for you.

And when you consider the choices, you realize that there really is no actual choice here to begin with.

You're going to do what he wants. Because you don't want to go to jail. You want to go home.

So here's my question for you: "Do you want to succeed ...or do you want to try and reinvent the wheel with your sales and marketing?" Because you can't be reading this book if things are already working out for you.

And they're probably not working because you were convinced somewhere along the way (by some guru, your ego, or something else) that you have to come up with some brilliant new way of selling what you've got.

You're trying to be original because EVERYONE tries to be original. And the confusing things is, yes - you DO need to be original. But your originality comes in when you differentiate your VALUE to the customer.

And that's perfectly fine. You want to stand out, after all. That's where the moves I mentioned in this book's subtitle will come in.

But you don't want to be 'original' in your actual sales process. Instead, you want to just take what already works, swallow your pride, win ...and ride that mechanical bull in your pink dress.

And in case you haven't figured it out yet, the sales process that works ...is in this book.

Make no mistake, the content you're about to read isn't just another set of re-hashed strategies. Instead, what you've got in your hands here is technology for sales and marketing success.

Let me say that one more time. It's technology. It's sales and marketing technology. That you can use. That you WILL use.

And to be certain this works for you, this content will all be presented in a system and sequence that you can follow for yourself in any industry (no matter how much you might be tempted to think your situation is different and doesn't apply to what I cover). I'll be giving you plenty of examples to show you how everything fits together.

# IT DOESN'T MATTER WHAT YOU'RE SELLING

If you doubt I can do this for you, think about this - you just bought my book, didn't you? Why do you think that is?

Do you think it was an accident that you bought it? Do you think it was an accident that you even found it?

Make no mistake, I set the conditions up so that this content would be placed directly in front of willing and eager customers who were specifically looking for the answers this book provides.

This is all on purpose. Keep reading and you'll see what I mean.

You're most likely going to get through this book very quickly. This isn't meant to be some 400 page odyssey.
I intentionally wanted to communicate these ideas and concepts as simply as possible. And I cut as much fat as I possibly could to get straight to the value for you.

As it is, you're drowning in information that you just don't need. You've been stuck in a cycle of information consumption that's been intentionally over-complicated in order to keep you buying more and more unnecessary products.

I'm choosing instead to give you something fast, engaging, useful, and actionable. Something that will get you to the results you've been looking for.

So ...don't expect this to be a very long read.

But because you'll probably get through it so easily, you might be tempted to move on and read another book after that.

DON'T DO IT.

In the words of the wise and oh-so-sultry Admiral Ackbar, "It's a trap!"

Like I said, you've been stuck in this cycle for way too long. It takes one to know one, believe you me, and my Amazon order history over the years tells the story of a guy obsessed with consuming information rather than using it.

I finally got my act together, but it took a while, and to this day, I'm still tempted to jump around.

But don't do what Andrew done did. Stick around instead.

Use what this book teaches you. Read it once all the way through, and then go back in and implement what you learn in YOUR actual business or sales job -- one chapter at a time. Do that, and your results will skyrocket. Your sales will peak. And your leads will come in hotter than a junkie's spoon. I kid you not.

And if you're wondering if I'm speaking truth here, I've got three final quick points to make before moving on.

# IT DOESN'T MATTER WHAT YOU'RE SELLING

1- You probably noticed that I saved the chapter on having a quality product for last. That's because I want to first give you a level of strategy you've never seen before.

That way, your eyes will be wide open when I get to that final key part.

But a quick spoiler for the end is that if you don't have actual quality behind whatever you're selling, these tactics will backfire on you and you'll have nothing but angry customers calling for your head.

On the other hand, having true value in whatever you end up selling will be like adding rocket fuel to your entire business model. It's that powerful.

2- There are always going to be tactics worth learning even after reading this book. I completely acknowledge that. In fact, when I work with my clients, we usually put together a core set of 5-10 tactics that will work best with their own personality and business model.

But there's a huge difference between using tactics as a crutch (and barely getting by) and using them as a baseball bat, knocking it out of the park, and tripling results overnight. And the difference is in whether they have the core methods you're going to learn in this book.

3- My prices are high. 90% of what I offer will run hundreds of dollars on the low end, and more likely, thousands for everything else.

And you usually can't even get access to certain things without first working with me.

I don't apologize for this.

Because I know that when people use what I give them, whether it's an info product, a one-on-one consultation, a group call, or anything else -- they get results. Plain and simple (we'll go more into that in the next chapter).

But I intentionally keep a few of my offerings like this one low cost. I do this so that even people who are short on funds can get a win. I also do this so that new potential clients can find their way to me without having to dig too hard.

But they're only going to come to me if I deliver value on every last thing I do, including this book. So if you don't believe in yourself yet (and we'll sort that out as well with what we've got in here), at least believe in my own selfish motivations.

I had to make what you hold in your hands HIGH IMPACT, or I'll never have people reaching out to do more business with me. This book represents my brand now.

And since I want to look good to y'all, it's probably time to throw a nice fat bonus your way.

With that in mind...

Social media. Don't you just love it? Isn't it great how we're all convinced that we have to be perfect at it? And how we have to spend all of our advertising money on it?

And how life is just incomplete if we don't have a profile and presence on every single platform?

Well, I don't know all about that. But I do know that whether you like it or not, there will come a time (if it hasn't happened already) where you find yourself desperately trying to engage at least some of your audience with it.

And if you're in the thick of it already, but aren't happy with your results, odds are pretty high that you're kinda doing it wrong. But never fear. It's 'Superstar' to the rescue with...*drum roll *...
"The Ultimate Social Media One-Two Punch."

While there's obviously more than one way to skin a cat, this special bonus breakdown will highlight two of the most powerful psychological strategies for getting a buyer's attention and slamming home their need for whatever product or service you're offering.

The cool thing about these two strategies is that each one alone can be very persuasive. But having one without the other leaves you open to making mistakes and looking way too one-dimensional to your audience. It's a tricky thing to try and balance your content when it's all coming from the same angle.

But putting these two strategies together into one combined marketing and sales approach will make you practically unstoppable.

Before today, you could only get this with a special one-time "Social Media Marketing" webinar ...that I ran for $200 ...that's no longer available. And now this book is the only way to get it.

So if you didn't go there already after I told you about it at the beginning of the book, head on over to www.ItDoesntMatterBook.com, where you can get this truly awesome resource along with bonuses on every other chapter to come. I know, I know. I'm awesome.

But you know what else is awesome? Your face. After turning the page. And moving on to one of the most important chapters you'll ever read about sales and marketing. Read on to learn about the magic of flawless positioning...

Oh, wait, I promised to reveal the number one reason peo will buy from you when all else is equal.

You didn't think I would forget about you, did you?

# It's because in THEIR mind, you WON'T be equal.

And THAT'S what this book is REALLY going to do for you.

With what you learn here, you'll make the key moves to put your product, your service, and yourself at the forefront of their mind when they're making the decision of who to go with.

No cheat codes needed.

Just straight up sales technique.

Accessible to beginners and pros alike.

Because I wasn't kidding here…

# It Doesn't Matter What You're Selling.

It just doesn't.

Not if you make the moves in this book.  Do that, and you'll make it rain.  You heard it here first.

Now let's get to it...

# Move 1: Position Yourself Flawlessly

I've got bad news for you:
People arc going to judge you no matter what you do.

BUT ...I've got some good news also:
People are going to judge you no matter what you do.

Yup. It can either be a good thing or a bad thing. It all depends on how you look at it. Or how you use it to your advantage.

Because bottom line, people judge. That's just how it works. It's an unconscious reflex that they couldn't turn off even if they wanted to.

And on the surface, this is probably a little scary to think about.

I mean, not being in control of something never feels good, right? But that's why this is actually good news. Because you DO have a certain measure of control here. You just need to know where it is.

You see, now that you realize that you can't stop people from judging you (or your product or service), you instead need to decide HOW they'll be doing it.

And this is where positioning comes in.

To give you a standard definition here, positioning is basically the place that your brand occupies in the mind of your customer. This can include you, your product, your service, your company, or all of the above.

It's basically how you distinguish yourself from competitors. But it's also how you're viewed even when you're not being compared to anyone or anything specific.

This is obviously about your image, but it also goes deeper than that. Sure, it comes down to who your customer thinks you are. But it also comes down to who YOU really are. It's affected by the market niche you choose to fill ...and how you choose to fill it.

It's the core foundation of everything else you do in your entire sales process. So if you don't have this part handled, everything else that you do will be inconsistent and unreliable.

This is about how you establish your identity (or the identity of your product or service) in the eyes of the purchaser.

It's one thing to have a reputation. It's another thing entirely to have people who have never heard of you before make instant assumptions about you.

And when your positioning is really dialed in, they'll make the exact judgements that YOU want them to make. Even on their very first experience with you.

How can this be done? Well, from the standpoint of coping with the world around them, people need to process countless bits of incoming information, and then classify all of it with zero delay.

As if your Facebook feed wasn't throwing enough at you, everywhere else you turn, there's this constant bombardment of information through advertising, work, friends, family, news, and just about anything else you can think of. And it's not going away any time soon.

And if people can't find an easy spot in their mind to associate any new info with, they usually discard it entirely.

Understanding this human tendency is the key to positioning yourself into common themes that people will easily understand.

But what you learn in this book will also help you make sure that the themes you attach yourself to specifically work to your advantage and make you more appealing.

You'll have authority in the eyes of your prospect.

And you'll therefore have the trust (that automatically goes along with this authority) that will help you sell way more easily, way more quickly, and at way higher price points.

We're talking about real value, of course, but we're also talking about perceived value.

In other words...

## WHAT'S IN IT FOR THE PROSPECT IF THEY BUY FROM YOU?

## AND, MORE IMPORTANTLY, ARE YOU MAKING THE ANSWER TO THAT QUESTION CLEAR AND OBVIOUS FOR THEM?

If you've positioned yourself well, not only are you viewed as unique, but the prospect can also articulate on some level WHY you stand out. They can describe you to their friends in a way that makes sense. They can compute in their own minds why buying from you is good for them in some way. And they come to the exact types of conclusions about these things that you want them to.

Want an obvious example? Take me. There's a real method to my madness, along with lessons to literally everything I do.

For example, I'll probably continue to experiment with different covers for this book, but the very first one I ever put out was designed to get the reader to jump to about 90 different conclusions about who I was BEFORE actually reading the book.

# IT DOESN'T MATTER WHAT YOU'RE SELLING

To paint the picture a little for you, that initial cover featured me in a loud pair of shades, an ace-of-reapers trucker hat, and a bright red leather jacket …holding up custom-made heavyweight championship belt.

A fucking championship belt. Are you kidding me? Anyone looking at that photo for the very first time was probably thinking something along the lines of "who the hell is this turd bag?"

But I did it as a lesson because I knew the content INSIDE the book would speak for itself and challenge the reader to reassess who they thought I was after they were done reading.

I got feedback from many of them telling me I was completely different than what they were expecting, and knowing this would happen, I instructed them in that first draft to break down the psychology of everything I did over the course of every chapter, and ask themselves:

1- Why I KNEW they would view me differently after reading
And
2- If I was so good at this whole sales and marketing thing, why I "let" them think those initial judgments about me in the first place.

(Spoiler: I wanted a vivid demonstration of how to purposely misdirect your audience before surprising them afterwards).

By the way, I wasn't being fake on the first cover; I was simply giving readers a specific (and real) side of me. I mention that because you'll need to be authentic on at least some level in your sales method, or the world will see right through you.

If you want to see the cover for yourself, I'll make sure to send it to anyone who grabs my other bonuses. Anyway, there are even more lessons in that cover. But let's not worry about that right now.

Let's just get you paid selling whatever you want to sell, regardless of your competition.

And let's do that by getting into an example that you were already familiar with before you ever found me. Let's talk about Mickey D's.

When McDonald's first got into business, they were NOT selling burgers and fries.

What they were selling instead was FAST FOOD. They were selling the speed and convenience of having that meal in your hands right after ordering. They were selling a new level of service that literally redefined people's lifestyles.

This is vital to think about because there's a very big chance you're marketing yourself as "burgers and fries" when you should instead be positioning yourself as "fast food."

# IT DOESN'T MATTER WHAT YOU'RE SELLING

And it could literally be costing you millions of dollars.

Getting back to me and that very first cover real quick, another part of my experiment was knowing that those readers were going to automatically imagine what my "voice" was like based on how I looked (which they'd "hear" in their head as they were reading).

And while the championship belt, the red leather jacket, and everything else automatically created certain judgments, I was doing a lot more beneath the surface with details such as the look on my face and my body language. I was sub-communicating a level of "self-assuredness" and certainty to the reader in a way that they didn't even consciously notice, which would help them give the content more of a chance rather than outright dismissing it.

The lesson was that there's often more to something than meets the eye, and I wanted those readers to really get that in their own experience. Call me biased, but the way I've always seen it is that this book is filled with gold from cover to cover. And since I knew that first cover would be a little controversial, in order to give readers the confidence to use it and succeed, I also had to sub-communicate that confidence in my face and body.

In other words, I wanted to make it clear to the reader that I still knew my shit and I could help them. That's was my positioning -- that I know my shit.

It's still authentic, but it's also a side of me I was deliberately sharing to offset the gaudy wardrobe. THIS is the level of thought you want to be on, even if you're not selling yourself.

I handicapped myself on purpose because you might be handicapped in a way that isn't in your control. So pay attention to what I'm saying here. This is where you serve YOUR customer...

Even if you work as a salesperson for some random appliance company out in middle America.

## MOLD WITH THE CLAY THAT'S ALREADY THERE

The basic approach you want to take in your positioning is NOT to create something new or different. Instead, you want to manipulate what's already in someone's mind.

Take connections that already exist in the customer's head, and tie them up differently. You'll accomplish a lot of this with subtlety. And then, in those times when you're way more direct, you'll have a lot more impact.

If you want a great example of how this is done, one of the best books for this is "The Game" by Neil Strauss. It's not a marketing book.

## IT DOESN'T MATTER WHAT YOU'RE SELLING

It's an autobiographical look at the author's two-year journey of going from completely clueless dork with no chance of getting a woman ...to self-assured, highly-attractive seduction artist.

The book follows him as he infiltrates an underground group of pickup artists, becomes one of them, learns their secrets --and then in true nerd fashion-- implements what he learns at a level nobody thought would be possible.

Now if you're looking for a debate on whether his behavior is acceptable or not, you're in the wrong book, buttercup. Regardless of whether I think it's right or wrong, all I care about is if you can learn from it.

And as far as truly high-level examples of positioning go, Strauss's story is absolute gold.

What does he do to position himself so well? He separates himself from the pack.

So when he first meets women, rather than telling them how hot they are (which would land him in the category of "every other guy out there"), he gives backhanded comments about their shoes. These little snips could almost be taken as an insult, which makes the women feel insecure and manipulates them into seeking his approval.

And when he thinks his main 'target' is losing interest, he quickly starts paying more attention to her friends instead, and let's the first one's pride and jealousy do the work for him.

If that isn't enough, when attractive girls compliment him, rather than bending over backwards to express how lucky he is to even be breathing the same air, he replies with a simple self-assured "humble" thank you.

These are all technically very subtle moves, so when he makes a more direct move of getting a phone number or arranging a date, these girls (who normally reject 90% of the guys around them) notice immediately and accept his invitation way more easily.

## PUBLIC SERVICE ANNOUNCEMENT: DON'T BE A DICK

Now just because I mention the effectiveness of Strauss's methods doesn't mean I suggest you treat your prospects like this.

It'll be a cold day in hell before I ever intentionally make one of my own clients feel like shit or play with their emotions in any way.

BUT you can still learn from this ...because things that you CAN do include:

- Flipping the script and doing the exact opposite of what the competition does.
- Doing the unexpected, which interrupts the other person's pattern and forces them to pay closer attention to you.
- Not giving your power away to your "prospect" (or anyone else, for that matter)

That last one is a key trap that most sales and marketing people often fall into. They give their power away. Don't let this be you.

What I mean here is that while I never play with the emotions of my own prospects, I also don't desperately chase them or frantically try to convince them to spend money on me. I just don't do it.

And I don't need to because what I have to offer them is truly valuable, so if they don't see that, it's fine because I'm too busy serving other clients to worry about it. I'm too focused on creating big wins for myself and the people already working with me.

And while I rarely give discounts, when I do offer some kind of deal, it needs to make sense, both for my business and my industry. It can't just be a cash grab. I actually gave price reductions to visitors of The Marketing Sales Superstar (my first podcast) as a reward for listening. And since you actually bought this book, you'd also get a better deal on my rates.

But the key part in my position (that I really want you to learn for your own advantage) is that the discount you'd get from me is never out of some need to get more paying customers.

Instead, it's because I want to add that extra layer of value to this book, which will increase its status, get more readers, and help me get my message out there (just like with my podcasts).

I say all of this because you want to make sure that when you give discounts, they actually make sense and they're NOT simply because you're desperate for more business.

If you're in an industry where discounts or "perks" are just part of the culture, that's fine -- but make sure the prospect still respects you. For example, if it's standard to go as low as 30% off, don't go down to 35. Word will get out, and then everyone else who bought from you will want to know why they didn't get the same deal. Trust me, I've seen it happen again and again.

Anyway, where I'm going with all of this is that you want to think about this mindset in both your sales and marketing because while you always want to respect the prospect (and, more importantly, serve them better than anyone else ever could), you never want to be needy.

Because in the end, looking desperate will only repel them.

Now one last point I want to make on this is that this doesn't mean you shouldn't try hard. All I'm saying is that if you're calling them over and over, your position needs to be:

"Look, I trust that this product is SO perfect for you, that I will not leave you alone until you at least give it a try."

And NOT

"Please, I really need to close X dollars in sales this month. Please buy this. I promise you'll like it."

See the difference?

It's all in how you position it.

## ANGLES OF POSITIONING

With that said, there are endless ways and countless angles you can go with in your positioning. It all comes down to how you establish your value in the eyes of the prospect.

One of the most powerful types of positioning that I've ever taught to clients is what's known as Price Anchoring. This is where you demonstrate (in NO uncertain terms) that the value of what you're offering is worth WAY more than what you're selling it for. And, if possible, the best way to do this is to anchor the value in their mind before you ever even reveal your final price.

Think about it. When you ask for $20K for your product or service, just about everyone's first instinct is to say no. And that's before they even get a chance to hear your pitch. But if you first establish that you're going to make them $500K off of their investment, all of a sudden, your price seems very fair when you reveal it.

There are a lot of great ways to go about this, and when I listen to my clients' sales call recordings, one of my favorite parts is showing them where they could have established this extra value BEFORE most of their product details even came up. And there are so many great ways to do it. But one of the easiest ways is through questions.

It's very simple. Rather than TELLING a prospect what something will be worth to them, ASK them what it could be worth.

Don't say "if you improve your results by just 2%, you'll make another $10,000 each month."

Instead, ASK: "if you could improve your results by just 2%, how much extra revenue would that bring in for you each month?"

When THEY'RE the ones speaking the benefits, it's coming from a much more trustworthy source.

And notice that the actual value of what you're offering didn't change here. But the perceived value shot straight through the roof. All by making them the bearer of good news instead of you.

This brings us to another great positioning angle. See, when they start answering questions like this, they also start filling in missing blanks about your offer (that you just haven't gotten to yet) to themselves as well.

It's simple -- since they feel good about everything they already know so far, their natural psychological instinct is to maintain that pattern and assume everything else is either just as good, or even better.

This is known as The Halo Effect. It's another thing I learned from Neil Strauss.

He was obviously selling 'himself' and there wasn't any exchange of money. But the concept worked all the same.

So again, in making sure he always stood out to the women he was interested in, when he'd go out to clubs, everything he did was the exact opposite of what every other typical beta male was doing.

Most guys led with a compliment about a woman's physical attractiveness. Strauss almost went as far as to make fun of them.

Most guys kept 100% of their attention on the girl they were interested in (which repelled her and killed any chance they had). Strauss would pay attention to her friend first, and often open the entire seduction process by completely ignoring the one he was really interested in.

As the one guy in the club who seemed to actually have self-value, he positioned himself as a better potential mate. One who would be able to cope with the harsh realities of the world and better ensure the survival and happiness of any children they might have.

He basically positioned himself as having the highest value in the entire crowd.

What happened was that these women saw SOME of the things he was doing (that made him seem like a better potential mate), and their brain categorized all the missing blanks as things that must be consistent with that way of being.

So even if they never saw him get into a fight, because their brain had to categorize him quickly and efficiently, all they could do on a first impression is assume that he could handle himself, even if he wasn't very muscular.

This isn't a suggestion that you trick your customer into spending money on you, but it is an invitation to find ways to put your best foot forward in your sales messaging.

And, since an overly-complicated message will turn the buyer off, this is also your reminder that you only need a very simple and direct method to close the sale.

Which brings us to another great type of positioning: Proof.

Imagine the following scenario.

You're a personal development expert.

You've written ten brilliant books. Your clients achieve massive results in very short periods of time. Sometimes you only need one phone call with them, and they report back just days later thanking you for helping them get a raise at work, lose those last five pounds, or quit smoking.

You even helped a billionaire find the love of his life.

In other words, you're the real deal.

This is awesome. It's so awesome, that some big time celebrity just emailed you a rave review.

Are you going to read it, shed a tear over the difference you're making, and then just move on with your life?

...OR are you going to ask his permission to include that email on your website and marketing?

If your product or service works as well as you say it does, get all the proof you can, and don't be shy about bragging to the world. You never know who's watching. And nothing does more for your message to the world than when an actual paying customer says they're happy with the deal they got.

Focusing on THEIR wins will lead to wins for YOU.

# FOCUS ON THE PROSPECT, NOT THE PRODUCT

Obviously the product itself is very important. So important that it's getting its own chapter later in the book. But when you're talking about your positioning specifically, everything comes down to the prospect.

Can you solve their problem? If the answer is yes, then all you need to do is communicate that to them in a simple, clear, and direct way.

And you do this by meeting them wherever they are in their own journey right now. I'll actually have some examples of that in the next chapter for you.

For now, just realize that your sales message is in its most potent form when it's speaking directly to the prospect from within the actual problem that they need to solve.

I mention this because most people hear this and think to themselves "I know this already," but then when you look at their marketing, they're not actually doing it. And yes, I mean you.

Okay, at this point, I think it's probably safe to say that you're reading the longest chapter in the entire book. But I'm really pouring a lot on here because this is the foundation of everything else you're going to learn. And it's going to play a part in everything else you do in your marketing and sales.

Before we move on, though, I've got just one or two more things I want to cover for you here. And the first one is about having a clear and concise sentence or two to sum up why your product or service is worth spending money on. Because remember...

## HOW YOU DO ANYTHING
## ...IS HOW YOU DO EVERYTHING

Your positioning is in everything that you say and everything that you do. That's why it's so important that you're genuine and authentic in your message and actions. If you want to be seen as a badass, don't just pretend to be one. Go and actually be one.

You should be able to take what you do or who you are, and be able to break it down to only one or two sentences.

Because we now live in a world where a goldfish's attention span is clocked at 8 seconds ...and a human being's clocks in at only 7 (I'm not being funny here, I actually read a study about this).

Our attention spans only widen AFTER we are intrigued or interested in something. But first, you have to make sure your positioning does your work for you. And a great way to do that is to measure how well you can communicate what you do in the confines of Facebook, Instagram, Twitter, or any other social media platforms.

Even if social media isn't part of your marketing or sales strategy, you should challenge yourself to make appealing profiles that position you well on each of those resources. This will also help you on LinkedIn.

So let's use Facebook Intros as an example.

I think they're only limited to 101 characters at this point. Not a lot of room to position yourself on the most viewed real estate in your entire profile (especially on mobile).

But let's look at how a few people that I know handle it...

## FACEBOOK INTRO EXAMPLES

# IT DOESN'T MATTER WHAT YOU'RE SELLING

My friend Paul used to run his own Martial Arts Gym. Now he helps others just like him achieve more success. His current intro on Facebook reads:

"I help Martial Arts Gym Owners Worldwide to get more Leads, Sales & find Profits in their gyms."

Not only is Paul the real deal and fully capable of getting other gym owners big wins, but he also knows exactly what it's like to be in their shoes, and he uses that in his messaging and positioning to them in everything that he does.

Facebook's intro leaves too little room for Paul to say that he's a been in that world himself, but everything else about his profile (including his posts and his photos) make it very clear he's one of them.

Next up is my friend Mike, known as "The Makeover Master." He specializes in revamping the business images of companies looking to take their branding to the next level.

His Facebook Intro reads:
"I Can Give Your Brand A Killer Makeover. I've Invested $200,000+ In My Skills, So You Don't Have To."

Then there's my friend Joey:
"High Ticket Email Copywriter. Performance Based Marketing Consultant. PRO Fish Taco Slayer."

Just like the expert copywriter that Joey is, he managed to communicate (in only about 100 characters):

- That he can handle high-ticket marketing campaigns
- That his fee is based on how well his work actually performs (so as a prospect, you know he's truly incentivized to do his absolute best work)
- That he's relaxed and has a sense of humor (with the whole fish taco joke)

I've got more for you...

My friend Carlos is an elite Direct Response Email Copywriter and Marketing Strategist.

His Facebook Intro:
"I write weapons grade copy. Have a list? Have an offer? Hate writing? Let's chat. See links (he then included downward arrow images)."

My friend Juliana:
"Soulful Marketing Strategist for High Achieving Female Entrepreneurs"

If that doesn't let her prospects know what they're in for, nothing will.

My friend Nick:
"I help Loan Officers attract 10 more Realtor partners by being themselves. LegionofLoanOfficers.com

(I LOVE how he fit his URL into his Intro despite Facebook's character limit)

Archer:
"I scale E-Commerce stores."

Diana:
"Dating coach, relationship expert and advisor to amazing men, women and couples worldwide."

Jason:
"I help businesses create and scale highly profitable ad campaigns."

What about me?
My own intro used to read:
"Putting your Sales Messaging and Marketing Strategy on STEROIDS! No needle required."

I then changed it to:
"Host of Shatter The Mold. "Your Sales and Marketing on steroids. No needle required."

By the time you read this, it will probably say:
"Host-Shatter The Mold. Author-It Doesn't Matter What
You're Selling."

Or if I'm feeling cute:
"Host-"Shatter The Mold." Author-"It Doesn't Matter What
You're Selling." Pimp."

Or if I don't want to let go of the whole steroid/needle joke,
"Author-Podcast Host-Strategist-Pimp. Putting Your Sales and
Marketing on Steroids-No Needle Required"

You'll notice these examples are more about a person's specific
branding, but you can easily do this for products or services as
well.

Here are some examples I'm just making up off the top of my
head:

"We make ergonomic beds that sooth your spine, relax your
body, and keep you well-rested through the night."

"Cloud storage you can count on in a flash. Unlimited storage
plans at super affordable prices. First 15GB free."

"Luxury Yoga Studio with top tier class options, experienced
instructors, and affordable entry programs for beginners."

But let's go even deeper and talk about how you can combine them both to really slam home authority by having a synergy between what you bring as a person WITH what your product or service brings to the table as well.

Take me, for instance. No matter what format you experience me in (my podcast, in-person coaching and consulting, high-ticket information products, live events, keynote speeches, or this book), my goal is to provide you with 10x the value that you pay for.

And that's at an absolute minimum. If I can control it at all, I'd rather you get 100x the value. Or even 1000x. Whatever I can do, I will do.

And that doesn't always necessarily mean that I need to shock or astonish you. I'm not trying to make this book longer. I'm trying to make it shorter. Because the fewer pages I can teach you in, the more refined and elegant my lessons are.

And because I don't need your experience of me to be the same in everything that I do, I can also have different types of positioning for each product or service I'm responsible for. READ THAT LAST SENTENCE ONE MORE TIME.

This is a huge key that you want to consider. Your position is only as good as the customer you're selling to. Some prospects have more money to spend than others. Some are more motivated.

If you can only serve one type, that's fine, as long as it's a deep market that you can work with year after year.

But if you're also able to position yourself in multiple directions and from different angles (without diluting your brand or your message), that's even better.

As long as there's a good reason behind any positioning that you do, it will always make sense, always serve your purpose, and always be something that your prospect will be pulled toward.

So when I say that I have different types of positioning for each product or service that I'm responsible, what I mean is this:

Anyone with an internet connection can listen to my podcast.

Anyone with ten bucks can get ahold of this book.

And hell, anyone with enough money can technically get in-person access to me as well.

But there's obviously more of a limit on that last one, because there's only one of me to go around.

And because there's only one of me, there's also only so much time in a day, week, or month to give to people. So you need much deeper pockets for in-person stuff than you did for the book.

But there are other levels of accessibility as well.

I've sold things for $97. I've also sold them for $500.

I've put things out there for everyone. And I've also offered exclusives to clients who work with me one-on-one.

In fact, my most popular offering, to date, is ironically the most difficult to get your hands on.

It's called The Baller Method. It's an online program with my absolute highest-impact marketing tactics.

It's my own personal playbook, so to speak, of getting sales for my business, along with getting results for clients that they never thought possible. Call me biased, but it's impossible to use the tactics in this program and not succeed in a huge way.

It actually used to be a special exclusive perk for clients who were with me for at least 6 months, but I later converted it into a stand-alone product.

And ...it's waiting list only.

That's right, if you want access to The Baller Method, you need to get on a waiting list first and hope that I release it again. Each time I put it out, I genuinely don't know if it will be the last.

Now with all of that said, let's look more closely at what's going on with this example and think about it more deeply, because there's a real lesson in what I'm doing here...

For starters, making this program scarce, from a tactical standpoint, automatically puts it more in demand. And it's an easy way to position your product or service as more valuable in the eyes of the prospect.

But remember how I said that your marketing and sales decisions need to make sense? That goes for this also, because sure, you can arbitrarily put anything you offer on some "made up" waiting list if you really want to. But with me and this specific product, I have an actual reason for doing it.

The reason for the waiting list is that there are unadvertised benefits and perks that people receive when they get The Baller Method that I always want to be real surprises for them. And to be honest, some of these bonuses are just way too fun to not do.

But even though I want these surprises for my customers, I never advertise what they specifically are because I keep updating and improving them, and I never want to make a promise that I can't keep on any bonus that I end up offering.

And yes, some of these extra surprises always seem to end up requiring my personal attention.

# IT DOESN'T MATTER WHAT YOU'RE SELLING

So with only one of me to go around, the last thing I want to do is take on 100 new customers with this product without knowing for sure if I can serve them all. And that's why it's waiting-list only.

Again, this is all part of my position when people work with me or buy from me.

They always get more than what they paid for.

Just look at all the bonuses you're getting with this book after only spending a few bucks on it. I'll count up everything for you in a later chapter, but you're basically getting perks that come close to $4,000 in value -- all free as a thank you for getting the book.

And in case it isn't clear, that's why people REALLY line up for things. That's the genuine 'non-tactical' reason why the right kind of product or service can be in such high demand.

But even so, nobody likes to wait for anything. So I really have to do the heavy lifting on my end, and make sure I'm actually someone who's worth waiting for.

There's a real level of psychology behind that. It's also another layer of my positioning...

Think about it. I force myself to rise to the occasion and over-deliver for my customer. Every single time.

They know I'm doing this and they hold me accountable.

And then they end up very happy with the results.

And then they buy from me again.

And then they tell their friends.

Learn from all of this.

Now, the rabbit hole goes even deeper. As of this writing, The Baller Method is not dramatically expensive. But as more and more people buy it, the price will continue to increase.

This ensures that early adopters get the most bang for their buck with way less competition knowing the very same tactics. And that becomes yet another good reason to buy it.

But this is all out in the open. I'm not "tricking" anyone into buying it.

They know full well what they're getting into, and they realize that the ultimate goal is a product they can use to skyrocket their own sales and marketing results.

I even make it a little extra difficult to buy it from me. Anyone who really wants a copy needs to request it, go through a brief application process, and THEN, depending on if they seem like solid action takers, they get on the waiting list.

# IT DOESN'T MATTER WHAT YOU'RE SELLING

Why do I put them through this when I know it'll deter some people from buying it (which will mean less money for me)?

It's another layer of positioning.  Because I know that if people spend money on something, but it's still too easy to get their hands on, they'll often put it on the shelf and neglect to actually use it.

And the information in The Baller Method is way too good to waste.

I ONLY want people buying it who will really use what's in it and actually make money off of it.  Their success with it leads to positive word-of-mouth about me and my products, and that leads to way bigger consultation deals for me and my company.

Making sense so far?  Okay then, on that note about bigger consultation deals, how about another layer of positioning?

As of this writing, if anyone wants to work with me in-person for a full week, I will fly out directly to wherever they are, and I'll give them as much attention and value as they can take.  But the fee for this in-person experience is $30,000.

Now regardless of whether you'd want to book me for that, all of a sudden, The Baller Method or any other deep-value high-impact products that I sell seem like way more of a steal.

So while The Baller Method is only a couple hundred bucks, even if it was $1,000 or even $2,000 (and one day, it probably will be), that still feels like a great deal considering all the value you actually get. Especially when you don't have 30K sitting around to learn this stuff from me in person.

Another layer to this is that unless you were already a client of mine, the only way you would have even heard of The Baller Method is by getting this book.

I don't advertise it.
I don't talk about it on my podcast.

Word gets around about it, and I can't control that, but otherwise, it's an insider secret, and I'm positioning just the knowledge of its existence as an added benefit to people spending their hard-earned cash on this book. At this point, I don't expect to talk about it in any other books I write.

BUT I'm also only sharing it with readers of this book because someone off the street (who doesn't learn what I'm teaching in these pages) wouldn't be ready for it anyway.

Sure, people usually jump straight to advanced levels once they go through it, but the entire foundation from this book is still needed.

Are you starting to see the whole chessboard here?

# IT DOESN'T MATTER WHAT YOU'RE SELLING

Everything I'm telling you in this chapter can be modified to serve your own specific purposes, regardless of whether you sell industrial-grade metals or fitness coaching for foodies.

Again, wrapping this all up into a nice neat bow, notice that while each of my products has their own positioning, they combine with each other and everything else I do to make up one entire giant position.

Within this position, I have the freedom and flexibility to make myself more available (when my products can serve more people at once) and less available (when certain products need more of my time and attention), depending on the situation.

My decision to do things like this allows the casual reader to get their hands on a book like this very easily (and put it to good use), and it also allows an even more serious segment of those readers to take a step beyond that and access my higher levels of content.

The key to this is actually making whatever I sell worth whatever someone spends on it (worth way more, actually).

So take my advice, and always over-deliver.

If this book was only a dollar, I'd want it to feel worth at least $20 to you.

At a bare minimum, you should be providing 10x the value that your customer is paying you for.

Because if you can't even do that, then your position has nothing behind it. And your brand and your business are worthless.

Now after all that Baller Method talk, it'd be a tab bit obnoxious to throw a link for you to buy it right now (even for me), but if you're really motivated to get your hands on it, and you want to get on the waiting list, I snuck a link to do so in the final chapter of this book. But read the book first. Get the value that's right in front of you. Don't get on that waiting list until you know for sure you can handle the content.

WHEW! Okay, I realize I just threw A LOT at you, and we really need to end this chapter and move on to everything else. But there's still more I wanted to cover around positioning for you.

So rather than force feed it into this part of the book, I went ahead and made it another bonus for you.

It's called "3 Power Moves to Positioning Your Brand for a Quantum Leap."

It details three key strategies that are designed for owning the conversation with the customer (by deploying sales conversion tactics that your competition is just too scared to use).

I'll open my playbook up even further for you, and give you a few of my favorite moves.

It's part of a program I'm putting together for clients-only that will cost around $149. But you get it free just for reading this book.

If you haven't done so already, head on over to
www.ItDoesntMatterBook.com,
where you can get your hands on it, along with every other bonus.

You're welcome.

Oh, and when you're done with that, turn the page already. You're about to learn how to grab your prospect's attention and never let it go again.

Let's get moving…

# Move 2: Put the Perfect Bait on the Biggest Hook

"I'm going to ask you one question, and all I want is a yes or no answer. Do you want to live through this?"

In just 24 words, Seth Gecko had his hostage Gloria's complete and undivided attention. And she was going absolutely nowhere.

It's an early scene from the 1996 movie "From Dusk Till Dawn" starring George Clooney as Seth. And the entire conversation only goes about one minute and fifteen seconds before Seth completely owns Gloria and has 100% control over her state of mind and focus of attention.

If you're curious, you can read the transcript of the entire conversation here: https://www.imdb.com/title/tt0116367/characters/nm0384936?ref_=tt_cl_tl2
...But it's even more powerful if you watch Clooney's delivery of the script in the movie itself.

Anyway, getting back to those first words of dialogue, if it were a sales situation with a prospect instead, some entrepreneurs might refer to this point of interaction as the 'hook'. But I like to call it the attention grab.

It's that critical point at the beginning of any real sales or marketing effort where your prospect notices you and needs to decide if you're interesting and relevant enough to keep paying attention to. It's the perfect bait on the biggest hook.

This is where headlines come in. Newspapers. Magazine covers. Facebook Ads. Anywhere you need to pull a potential customer in and get them to read more.

This is also where those critical first few seconds of a cold call come in, and you need your target to stay on the line.
Or it's whatever you say when you're face-to-face with someone you want to sell to, and you're shaking their hand for the very first time.

It's your way into the sale. And as you can tell from Seth's talk with Gloria, it's all about frame control. You've got a specific reaction that you're looking for the prospect to have. A certain action you want them to take. A certain way you want them to feel. And you socially engineer your way to whatever that is by the attention grab that you use on them.

Seth didn't stop at asking Gloria if she wanted to live. He got her to say 'yes' and THEN said more to her based on that. The implication of every other part of the talk was "Okay, fine, if you want to live, here's what I need from you."

He then started giving her rules. He needed to control his hostage, right? His first rule was no noise. And no questions.

He pulled out his gun and told her that if she makes a noise, "Mister .44 makes a noise." And if she asked any questions, "Mister .44 answers it."

The gun was now the central point of where he wanted her attention, so he kept it that way through the entire list of rules. The last rule was to not run. Because if she did, Seth had "six little friends, and they can all run faster than you." He told her this as he was holding the loaded gun to her head.

This is another example of solid positioning, by the way.

Seth's the guy who decides whether Gloria lives or dies. That sort of makes everything else he says to her very, very important.

And while that first question that he chose to ask her was important, it's really who he was (as a person) that made it mean something.

It's the fact that he's really a stone cold killer, and she can see this clearly about him. That's why she takes his question very seriously to begin with and actually believes him.

Remember how I said that every concept here is linked? I wasn't kidding. It's all one big recipe for sales and marketing success. And every new ingredient makes the bread rise even higher.

Now you're probably not going to want to hold a gun to your prospect's head in order to get them to buy something for you. I've heard rumors here and there that those types of decisions lead to jail time and all sorts of other minor disruptions to your life.

But you want to do everything in your power to have them paying as much attention to you as possible ...without them also feeling like you might kill them in about five minutes.

And as a quick side note, Seth's decision to kick things off with a question that Gloria would automatically answer in a predictable way is a very high-level tactic that's used by Direct Response Copywriters all the time.

Whenever I work with clients on refining their sales messaging and really pushing the limits on how much money they can make, this is one of the first topics I cover with them, because it's very easy to learn and it helps them boost their sales conversions with killer precision.

So don't take what Seth did there lightly.

Anyway, since you might not have a loaded gun on hand, here's an easy guideline to making high-impact attention grabs at will:

Put simply, your 'attention grab' needs to speak to the self-interest of your prospect ...in whatever way your product or service will actually help them.

Some attention grabs will be more obvious. Some less. Some will be more direct. Others indirect. Either way, the mindset of what you're doing is always the same.

## GRAB THEIR ATTENTION
## EVERY CHANCE YOU GET

You want attention grabs in every part of your sales messaging, every part of your marketing, and every part of your overall presentation.

You want them in your headlines. You want them in your calls-to-action. You want them in every question you ask.

You want them everywhere possible, because you want to be engaging. You want to be interesting. You want to make people curious about you and your product … all while they're simultaneously seeing you as the person who can solve that problem (if only they pay closer attention and buy from you).

This isn't even always about making a specific sale, by the way. It's about getting a reaction that you're looking for. Or some other result that doesn't necessarily involve the customer parting with their cash.

Take this book, for example. Okay, you bought it. The transaction is complete. I won, right? Well, not according to my definition of winning. If all I wanted was for you to buy this book and do nothing else, I'd be very short-sighted.

No, what I want is so much more for both you AND me. I want you to read the whole thing. I want you to absolutely love it. I want you to tell your friends and leave a five star review on Amazon (read that last sentence a few times).

And none of that happens if you buy this book, read ten pages, and then stuff it somewhere out of sight on your bookshelf.

So I need to keep you engaged. I need to spike your interest in some way throughout the entire book.

I especially need to hook you at the very beginning and very end of each chapter.

Notice how I do that.

Notice how I start each chapter with either something controversial enough to stop you in your tracks ...or something that makes you wonder and want to hear more ...or (when I'm really at my best) something with an implied promise of what you will get by continuing to read.

Whatever it takes. Because if I don't have your attention, I don't have anything else.

# ATTENTION IS THE MOST SCARCE (AND VALUABLE) RESOURCE

When it comes to marketing or selling to your consumer, make no mistake: Attention is the most scarce resource you're ever going to be after.

In today's "stare at my phone/scroll through Facebook/laugh at cat videos" culture, you are literally battling with every possible distraction out there. And you need to hold the attention of your prospect longer than anything else they've got coming at them whenever they read your ad, answer your call, or get your email.

How important is the attention grab to your process? So important that I've had clients admit to me that they first signed up for emails from me just to study how I'm handling my own engagement, and copy what I'm doing (my own follow-up strategies, how I deliver products, etc.).

Now having people rip off my style isn't exactly the most flattering thing in the world, but it's at least nice to know that they understand how vital this step really is.

## EVERY PART OF YOUR MESSAGE, BOTH ONLINE AND OFFLINE, SHOULD BE ABOUT GRABBING ATTENTION

When you go to a website that's specifically selling a unique product or service, it's almost always obvious whether the site is old or not. You can instantly tell by the look, structure, and general feel of it.

On a certain level, "websites" are obsolete. They're bad for business. They were designed for people who still had time to futz around online and poke through a site with nothing better to do. But now that they have funny cat videos waiting for them, and now that they're kind of over the whole fancy website trend, there's just no point anymore.

All that the older websites do is force the prospect to work harder to find the part of the site where they can actually spend money and solve a problem of theirs. This causes nothing but confusion. And remember, a confused mind always says no.

Look at movies as a clear example of this. They don't even have their own websites anymore.

All they really have are their profiles on Facebook, Instagram, and Twitter. That's all they need.

And that should really tell you something.

This doesn't necessarily mean that you shouldn't have one. There are still industries and market niches where having a robust website is expected.

BUT - the fact that it's not required everywhere should really be pointing you in a direction where you're being way more intentional about how you're guiding visitors through their online experience with you.

# IT DOESN'T MATTER WHAT YOU'RE SELLING

This is where sales funnels come in. Rather than have countless sections and multiple exit points, these are stripped-down versions of websites that are designed with the very specific goal of visitors taking very few and very clear actions toward an eventual sale.

A typical funnel has an attention grab as it's headline, with a promise of giving the site visitor some kind of benefit (an answer to a burning question, a solution to a big problem, a free sample of something, etc.).

It then asks the visitor to provide an email address to send the promised 'prize' to (now they have your email and can market to you for free instead of spending more money on ads).

You give the email, and all of a sudden, you're most likely on a new page with another attention grab and a sales pitch for something. Maybe even after you buy, you're then directed to an upsell for another item. Again, it's all very intentional, very specific, and very direct.

Whether or not this is something that will work specifically for you, the fact still remains - this method of selling WORKS.

And the whole foundation for its success is in the attention grabs on each new page that you're directed to. Without them, the visitor doesn't pay attention, take action, or make any purchase.

And since it works so well -- even if you don't have an actual funnel (or need one just yet), you still want to adjust your approach to behave like one as much as possible. You want attention grabs in every step of your sales process -- little hooks that will move the conversation with the prospect forward and make the sale.

You want an attention grab in your headline, in the first thing you say on the phone, or when you meet someone face-to-face. You want an attention grab before you introduce what you're selling. You want an attention grab in your call to action. You want it everywhere. You want your prospect's attention 100% fixated on you all the way through until you've finally completed that sale.

Now at this point in the chapter, it might seem like I'm beating a dead horse here. But I'm really pushing this button on you hard because this is such a crucial part of the sales process that people always seem to overlook -- EVEN WHEN they know it's important. It's more important than you realize, and it will make you more money than you could ever imagine.

I've got countless stories of people who learned this one key tactic and had their business blowing up within 30 days. Some in as little as 7 days!

If that sounds like something you might enjoy yourself, another thing to keep in mind here is that your attention grab should be able to transcend any format.

In other words, if you can put it in a headline, you should just as easily be able to say roughly the same thing in a conversation.

For Example:
"Wouldn't it be amazing if you could straighten and whiten your teeth in only 4 weeks -- without any extended dentist visits or long drawn out treatments?"

If my teeth are crooked and a tab bit yellow from all that coffee I've been programmed to consume, the above sentence would definitely grab my attention - especially if it's believable.

So if it's in an ad, you can include a testimonial of a real person with their photo. And if it's in a conversation, the credibility is implied by talking about your "friend Steve, who didn't believe it for a second but gave it a try anyway (since they were offering a 60-day no-questions-asked money back guarantee) ...and boy, is he happy that he did!"

## IF IT GRABS ATTENTION
## ...IT'S AN ATTENTION GRAB

We aren't only necessarily talking about the words we use here. Images also work. Or online video demonstrations. Or experiences for attendees at live events or trade shows. Or stories that you tell (more on that in the next chapter). Or anything else. Don't limit yourself in where you can go with this. You're sitting on a lot of opportunity here. You just don't realize it yet.

Remember last chapter where I mentioned meeting them wherever they are in their own journey RIGHT NOW?

Well, you'll see more of this when we get into stories, but since this strategy also includes relatable attention grabs, let's look at a few examples right now.

Notice that these examples have positioning built into them as well (it's all connected). See if you can spot that in them:

"Jane was having trouble booking clients, and she always seemed to be stuck living month-to-month, barely scraping by. She needed to multiply her revenue by at least 3x if she was going to gain any traction. So she hired Andrew to work with her on a new marketing strategy."

"Mike couldn't meet a girl to save his life. He was frustrated, confused, and had been desperately trying for years. He knew he could never just walk up to someone, even though he wished he could find a way to make it easy. Then he discovered Dave's "Attraction Secrets" book."

Notice how they're structured to speak directly to the person who's CURRENTLY having a problem. And how they only need a very small amount of vivid detail to paint the picture of what's going on. And how they're simultaneously implying that the action each person took (which, in your specific case, would be them buying from YOU) was the key to finally solving things.

And from an attention grab standpoint, notice how relevant they are to the person's problem.

Here's another one:

"No matter what he did, Joe just couldn't get people to sign up for his service without complaining about his price and demanding a better rate. So he used Andrew's "Objection Obliteration Method" and started learning about their deepest business needs and most desired financial upside BEFORE quoting them a price."

Notice that this one is a little different, but still brief. It actually spells out the "What" solution to the prospect (i.e. what they actually did), but with built-in curiosity since the "How" was still missing (i.e. how they actually did it).

If the "what" makes enough logical sense to the prospect, and they're in enough pain and frustration over the issue that's being described, there's no way they're not going to want to learn more and find out the "how" behind the solution. That in and off itself grabs their attention.

Regardless of how simple this might seem on the surface, this type of messaging has a lot more power behind it than you might realize. After all, whatever it is that you offer might not seem like that big of a deal to you. For you, it's an easy solution to provide.

But for people who don't know how to do what you do, or have never had access to the type of product you offer, this is way more impressive to them than they even consciously realize.

Remember, YOU'RE not the one buying it, so don't underestimate the power behind whatever it is that you're selling. Instead, ask yourself: "What does the CUSTOMER see as valuable?" That's exactly the kind of thing that will have their attention.

With all of that said, let's talk about the best ways of getting inside the prospect's head so that you can sell most easily to them...

## HOW TO CREATE THE BEST ATTENTION GRABS

Here's the part of the chapter you've really been waiting for (that sentence is an attention grab). ...But let's first get something straight right now, you friggin' egotistical muffin top. You are NOT creative enough to make a million bucks using your perspective alone.

As the seller, you're simply not as in-tune with the needs of your prospect as you'd like to think you are.

But your market is.

So whether you talk to them directly OR you simply try your best to look at things from what you think their perspective is...let THEM do the heavy lifting here. Let them tell you the best way to hold their attention long enough to pull their wallets out.

All you need to do is ask the right questions.

Some questions you can answer for yourself as long as you're looking at them as an actual prospect. Some of them you might actually have to chat with customers (which is always a great move, if you can do it). Some will be easier to answer. And some will be more difficult. But once you start to really get answers that truly speak to the wants and needs of your consumers, money will roll in faster than you can count it.

With that in mind, here are three of my favorite questions to ask (that really go deep into the buyer's psychology):

Key Question 1:
"If your prospect could wave a magic wand to change anything about their problem, what would they change?"

It's very possible that your product or service already addresses EXACTLY what your prospect TRULY wants, but it's so basic and simple, you didn't think to feature it as a key part of your sales message.

It's also possible that your product or service isn't addressing what your prospect really wants, but you could change that if only you knew that's what they wanted. Bottom line, you want what you're offering to literally feel like magic to the people you're selling it to.

You literally want to be the answer to their prayers.

But until you know what they'd actually wave their wand at, you're leaving a LOT of money on the table without even realizing it.

And speaking of not realizing something…

Key Question 2:
"What do prospects want that they would never admit to out loud?"

This is a great question that I learned from a famous copywriter named Mitch Miller. In Mitch's main example of how this might come into play, he used Home Surveillance as a commodity that's purchased for reasons that most people don't realize or admit to.

The companies that sell this focus on protection, peace of mind, safety, and easy setup. And that's fine and all.

Beneath the surface, though, people fantasize about catching a thief in the act, keeping their spouses from cheating, and having more status among their neighbors (if the brand they use is fancy enough).

Home Security Companies that want to capitalize on those reasons obviously can't just come out and say them. It's way too taboo, and the last thing people want to do is acknowledge their hidden reasons for doing something.

But what these companies can do is address and highlight these things through storytelling in their marketing campaigns. More on storytelling next chapter! But first, we've got one more...

Key Question 3:
"What solutions do consumers in your market already spend the most money on?"

No vote on this entire planet is more valid than one that's already being made with someone's wallet. If people are already spending their money somewhere, that's your sign that there's more money to be made.

The only question is how you position yourself around what they already want. But before you can even start to position yourself the right way, you need make sure they're spending money in an area that you can serve them.

And that's what this question is all about.

Anyway, those are three of my favorite questions to ask when I'm trying to come up with high-impact attention grabs.

If you like those, I've actually got a full list of 12 core questions that I always answer for myself before marketing anything, no matter how much experience in the market I already think I have.

Do you want the whole list?

Well, it's $97.
Okay, not really. See, they were a bonus on a program that I used to sell for $97.

But the price you need to pay for this list?
$0.
Nada.
Nothing.
Zilch.

The list is now yours free-of charge as a thank you for picking up this book. It's one of the bonus resources I mentioned earlier. You can go ahead and get your grubby little paws on it by going to www.ItDoesntMatterBook.com.

Anyway, before moving on to the next chapter, here are a few more quick tips to help you with all of this:

# IT DOESN'T MATTER WHAT YOU'RE SELLING

Tip 1- Do your research into the sales and marketing messaging of your competitors. Ask yourself why certain ads or banners got your attention. Was it a headline? An image? Does it touch on an emotion? If yes, in what way?

Learn from whatever insight this research gives you.

Tip 2- Think of movie trailers. Why do they get people so excited to see the whole film? Do you notice how they don't give it all away? How they keep you curious? How they give you a glimpse of what you'll enjoy when you actually pay?

Notice how they sort of tease you and leave an open loop that can't be closed unless you buy a ticket and see the whole movie? Learn from this.

Tip 3 - "Throw rocks at your enemies." If there's something about your market that you stand against, don't be shy about it.

Whatever it is that you're sick of might be something your prospects are sick of as well.

There's a chain of used car dealerships that take all the hassle out of buying your car from you if you'd like to sell it. I think it's called WeBuyCars, but don't hold me to that.

Anyway, the company is growing like crazy because it's leveraging people's resistance to haggling with crooked used cars salesmen.

Are all used car salesmen crooked? Of course not, but there's a stigma there that's really got a hold of the market.

But by positioning themselves as a used car buying option that protects the consumer from that 'evil' conniving sales guy, this company is throwing rocks at a common enemy and galvanizing prospects into doing lots of business with them. Learn from this.

On that note, remember - Your attention grabs need to speak to the self-interests of the prospect in whatever way your product or service will actually address them.

Accomplish that, and you'll be richer than a truck full of marzipan.

Okay, it's storytime. Literally. Turn the page, and learn about one of the most lethal weapons in the world of sales and marketing…

# Move 3: Build Intrigue with the Right Kind of Story

When it comes to sales and marketing, do you ever feel like it's you AGAINST your prospect?

If you said yes, there are a few reasons for this. And one I hear often from clients is how frustrated they are that the prospect just doesn't understand how valuable or useful the product is.

There's a very easy fix to this, and I'll explain with a quick story about Mark, Linda, and Andrew.

Mark ran a struggling yoga studio.
Andrew was a marketing consultant who could help.
Mark's wife Linda was the smart one. She saw how tough Mark had it, and found Andrew so he could fix things.

So Andrew reviewed Mark's sales funnel, worked a few parts out in his head, and told Mark it would cost $8,000 to go in and fix everything.

And Mark was sad.
Very, very sad.

See, he didn't want to spend $8K fixing this. That was just too expensive. And for what?

A few days of Andrew telling Mark how he sucked at his job and couldn't get a customer if his life depended on it?

No, thank you, sir.

But there was a silver lining to this. Andrew took one look at how Mark and Linda acted around one another, and quickly realized Mark wasn't really in charge anyway.

So Andrew went and convinced Linda to hire him instead. And then she ...ahem… "convinced" Mark that this had to be done (that's code for "she made him do it").

So ...Mark was still sad.
Andrew was now glad.
And Linda was like, "oh, Marky, it's not that bad."

Anyhoo, Andrew went straight to work on this. In the span of a few days, he mapped out four choke points that Mark had in the business. He fixed three of them, and completely got rid of the other one.

Two months later, Mark had profited in excess of $93,000. And Andrew was like, "I told you so, Marky."

Now I ask you. Would YOU trade eight grand for a profit of ninety-three? I know I would.

More importantly, does $8,000 seem as painful to spend now?

Hell, what if it was discounted to $6,000 under the condition that the client took action on what he was told, promised to refer new customers if everything worked out, and committed to doing EXACTLY what Andrew told him?

Now, not only are you making $93 G's, but you're saving $2,000 on top of that!

If that kind of deal is wrong, then I don't want to be right.

## SO WHAT JUST HAPPENED?

Let's break down what just happened here. I actually threw in a little extra sales psychology with the whole $2K discount (if you can't do that in your situation, just 'price' yourself higher knowing you'll drop to the real price when it's time to close things up).

But the key take away I want you to have is that it was much easier and way more impactful to describe what I can do with my service through a STORY.

## WHY STORIES ARE VITAL TO YOUR SALES AND MARKETING

Why exactly are stories so powerful? Well, think about the biology and psychology of people. While we're highly evolved compared to where we were when things began, we're still animals on some very basic and important levels.

There's a reptile part of our brain that drives our instincts and has one purpose in mind: Survival.

Our subconscious processes everything we experience at speeds that we don't even perceive. And in order to do this, it must take any new information we encounter and instantly decide how to classify it.

Because of this fact, every successful sale requires two types of introductions:

1-You (or whoever/whatever is selling for you)

And

2-Whatever it is that you're selling

It doesn't matter whether it's face-to-face, over email, on the phone, or any other type of communication. The seller and what they're selling need to be "introduced" and put up for review in front of the prospect's reptile mind.

And to put it to you without any sugar-coating, whenever your brain is introduced to ANYTHING new, it always asks itself: "What is this? Do I eat it, fight it, fuck it, or run from it? Am I safe? Am I in danger? Do I want this? Who is this person who is selling this to me? What is this thing they are selling?"

You get the idea.

And because you're walking into this situation as a complete unknown to your prospect, you have to find an efficient and effective way to answer those questions, or you'll blow the entire sale.

The reason it's so important to have stories for the prospect at the beginning of their experience with you is because from early childhood, we're used to hearing stories from all sorts of different authorities in our lives.

Parents. Books. Television.

As children, we take any and all information in without question, so all of these sources condition us to drop our guard whenever that information is being presented in a story format.

So when YOU'RE telling a story to someone else, it's subconsciously amplifying your value. It's raising your status in their eyes.

It's making you an authority, which highlights who you are and enhances what you're offering in the prospect's mind. This, in turn, manufactures trust and familiarity. They feel like they know you better and are automatically more comfortable with you.

There's no way around it. It's human nature.

And if you're aware of this, you're in a position to craft stories that will drive home whatever point you're looking to make in your prospect's mind.

The work I've done with clients on this part of the sale has been some of the most invigorating because we get to delve into the history of the product or person and come up with some really interesting gems that seamlessly work their way into whatever format the sales presentation is taking.

This is why people who market their products online through several steps in a sales funnel have trouble if there aren't any stories in their sequence.

This is also why a lot of sales presentations fall flat.

It's as simple as this - The better the story you tell, the easier it is for you to sell.

It's simple math: If hearing a story is already making the prospect's mind more receptive ...AND if you're then structuring the story in a way that says good things about you or the thing that you're selling -- you end up easily increasing your own value in their hearts and minds without any real effort.

## INFORMATION IS NOT ENOUGH.
## YOU NEED EMOTION.

But it goes deeper than that. Think back to a long speech you sat through at some point in your life on some subject you couldn't care less about. What was the missing piece in the speech maker's presentation?

Emotion.

Without emotion, people don't notice you. They don't respond. They don't take action. They don't care.

And stories are a wonderfully easy way of accessing the emotions of the listener.

I remember watching a presentation by a vegan who was using storytelling to make his case against eating meat. He was so vivid and descriptive in his examples, you couldn't help but be affected, even if you disagreed with him. He just did such a great job of putting you there emotionally.

At one point, he had the audience look at their hands as he asked them "do these look like effective tools for mauling a pig? I've put my hands on pigs, and they've instinctively rolled over so I could rub their bellies."

Notice how he associates his interaction with the pig as if it's a pet -- like a cat or dog that you love. All of a sudden that pig that you were about to eat is a member of the family.

The presenter continues, "now say you've killed the pig. Now it's carcass is open. Are you going to eat the organs? The ligaments? All the extra bits?"

Now you're visualizing this raw dead body. Blood and guts everywhere.

Now he's got you a little nauseous. And that's when he asks in his thick British accent:

"Are you 'off your food' now? Because that's exactly what people tell me when I describe this for them. But why do they react this way? Is this the reaction of someone who nature intended to be a meat eater???"

Now, this is obviously a topic that can go in a million different directions, and I'd much rather show you how to line your pockets with cash from your sales and marketing.

But I wanted to highlight this example for you, whether you agree with the presenter or not, to show you how emotions can be manipulated to drive home a point or fix someone's attention on something. It's a very powerful tool that most people either ignore or only get very little use out of.

You need people to feel something so that they consciously engage more. Why do you think most people have so much trouble focusing in school?

It's because the brain just isn't designed to have an endless stream of information spoon fed to it non-stop without having anything to relate it to in the process.

This is also why listing the features of something without finding a way to communicate the corresponding benefits usually kills the sale.

# NO STORY, NO SALE

How effective is a story? So effective that Mark and Linda from the beginning of this chapter aren't even real, and those things I said about them didn't even happen.

But the details, pacing, and structure of that story completely changed how you thought about me AND what I offer, right?

That's how powerful this stuff is. And it wasn't even that good of a story! Imagine how powerful you can make your message when you have a story behind it that's actually good.

And yes, I know you're doubting yourself right now, but trust me -- it's very easy to tell good stories once you understand the psychology behind them. I wouldn't tell you this if it wasn't true.

It's not hard to learn the psychology behind them either - I'm dropping tons of insights and tips in these chapters and the bonuses that accompany them.

All you need to do is review what I'm giving you and try it out. You should have everything you need here to get moving.

With that said...

HUGE INTEGRITY NOTE - While something similar to the Mark-Linda story may or may not have happened (I'll let you decide what you think is true), I didn't want to share actual (and confidential) client info in a mass-produced book. And rather than deceive you, I came clean about it right away.

But when you sell your stuff, you need to tell TRUE stories. If you don't, some not-so-friendly government folks might be unhappy with you, and that's never an easy conversation. You've been warned.

Anyway, the lesson here is that you should have a full arsenal of stories to deploy in just about any sales or marketing situation you're faced with.

You want:

- Stories that wipe out price objections.
- Stories that illustrate how well your product works.
- Stories the tell the prospect how easy it is to follow your system.
- Stories that demonstrate your expertise.
- Stories that deliver social proof.
- Etc.

Most importantly, you want a story that explains why you're selling whatever it is that you're selling. And if you don't have a story like that, you should at least have one of why people buy it.

And if you don't have any stories yet? Easy - borrow someone else's. YOU don't have to be in the story for it to be effective. For example, if you're the new salesperson for a software company, make friends with your colleagues and ask them about their favorite customer success moments.

Hell, this is something you should be asking your hiring manager about before you even take the job.

And if you're running your own show, you have absolutely no excuse for not having stories that drive home the value of what you're offering.

## STORIES ARE WAY MORE IMPORTANT THAN YOU'LL EVER REALIZE

I've had people reach out to me when they were starting a new sales job or business JUST to help them craft stories with the right kind of psychology and pacing. THAT'S how important they are.

And in case you haven't figured it out yet, you're not a unique or special snowflake. So if you think stories won't work for you or YOUR situation, you're wrong, fool. You're just wrong.

This works for anyone, so if you're a plumber, tell a story about how you saved someone's basement after a pipe burst and they needed immediate help.

If you're selling a SAAS product, tell a story about how using it saved someone's job (preferably someone with the same job title as the person you're pitching to).

If you're selling an info product, tell a story on how it improved someone's life, even if that life was your own.

I remember a friend of mine who had a fencing company telling me about one of his first customers. She was old, cranky, miserable, impossible to deal with, and extremely impatient. The worst part was that because he was so new to the game, he didn't realize how certain weather issues would affect the work, and he had to return numerous times to fix her gate.

But he did it. He kept going back without charging her a single extra penny. And despite this, she was cruel and would berate him non-stop. But he had made a guarantee of quality, and he lived up to it.

What's the point here? Well, when he was more experienced, and he was in front of a much more lucrative opportunity, the prospect was very hesitant about spending so much money. But the deal would have made my friend's entire fiscal quarter if he could just close it.

So what did he do?  He gave the prospect the phone number of the mean old lady who hated him, and said this:

"Call her.  If you ask her what she thinks of me, she'll probably call me an asshole and tell you how much she hates me.  But one thing she CAN'T tell you is that I did a bad job or wasn't there for her.  I lived up to my guarantee to her despite all the abuse.  And I'll do the same for you."

The prospect signed up the next day.  Why?

Because my friend had a visceral and powerful story that demonstrated his ability to deliver on his promise, which was the only thing holding them back from moving forward in the first place.

Remember near the beginning of the book where I said that it's sometimes simply about getting the prospect past their fear?  This is what I was talking about.

Think hard on all of this because even moments that feel like failures or are frustrating in some way can become useful stories that bring you more success.  Just like with my friend and that mean old fart of a woman.

Because ultimately, you're using stories to answer one important question:

## WHY SHOULD THEY CARE?

In case it isn't clear from the examples above, the number one question you need to answer in your stories is "why should they care?"

Why should the prospect care about you? Why should they care about what you're selling? What should they care about anything you have to say?

The answer here is that they only care about themselves.

And that's okay. There's no need to fault them for being human. But what you need to do is realize this is happening and make sure your story has some way of communicating what's in it for them, whether you're telling them directly or indirectly.

Either way, you have to connect. And a great way to make sure your story connects with them is to simply figure out where a customer is at "now" in their journey, and craft a story based on THAT. For example, if you sell debt consolidation, you want stories about people with their backs against the wall.

Because those are the people who will be calling you.

If you sell software, you want to take the problem that the software is designed to solve, and you want to tell stories about people who still have that problem, but are fixing it with your product or service. And you want to be painfully vivid and really push whatever button's really got them unhappy.

Whatever the issue, cater the details and flow of your story to match and resonate with it.

Want a pro tip on this? Hardly anyone uses it, but it works better than a blue pill on date night:

Use Google to find articles or forums of people describing what it's like to have whatever problem their having, and then use THEIR WORDING in your ad copy or sales presentation. There's no better way to guarantee that your stories will be speaking directly to their pain and connect with them way more intimately.

And in case you haven't figured it out yet...

## THIS WORKS FOR BOTH
## LITTLE AND BIG FISH

You're probably familiar with Salesforce.com. If you're curious how they turned into a billion dollar company, there's a well-known book that covers the journey, titled "Behind the Cloud."

And one of the most interesting things covered in the book was how the people at Salesforce always had a brand-friendly and relevant story available whenever the press was around. After all, what better form of distribution is there than the mass media -- especially when they aren't even charging for the spotlight their articles provide?

Salesforce understood this very well. They realized that without an interesting story to push their narrative, they never would have grown so quickly. So they positioned themselves very strategically from day one.

Learn from their success. You might be surprised by how well you do.

Anyway, before we move on, there's one more key point to make about all of this…

## STORIES DO MORE FOR YOU THAN MAKE JUST ONE SALE AT A TIME

Your stories are not just about getting people to buy from you. They're also about getting them to take action.

And they're about getting them to make good choices. And about helping them get true value out of what you're selling.

After all, if you're selling an exercise program, you don't just want people to buy from you and be done with it. You want them to buy from you, use the program, achieve mind-blowing results, rave about you to their friends, give you a testimonial, offer you their first born (okay, maybe not that last one), AND… wait for it… BUY FROM YOU AGAIN, you damn knucklehead!

What, you don't think I have more books on the way after this one? Know this - EVERYTHING I do (including the book you now hold in your hands) MUST be awesome. I won't let it be anything less.

Because I know that if this book is even half as good as I want it to be, then your decision to part with another nine or ten bucks a year from now for another one will be the easiest decision of your day.

If I told you that some of my most lucrative sales came through telling stories, would that surprise you? And would it surprise you to hear that those people then became additional success stories themselves? And that those stories brought me more customers? And that this is my sales cycle in a nutshell?

You may not start things off with a story about someone saving their business when they only had 30 days before being evicted. But stay in this game long enough, and you will.

And in the meantime, work with what you've already got.

Because it will be the wins you get for your customers that motivate you to do an even better job for the next person you sell to after that. Because you realize that being able to tell prospects about your prior successes is exactly what will make getting that new sale easier than a nymphomaniac on coke.

That's the power of stories in sales.

And if that doesn't convince you of how vital stories are to making money, know this. I have an exclusive product for my high-end clients (that I'll one day make available to the general public) that's specifically geared around using stories to obliterate every last objection to a sale ...BEFORE the objection even comes up! And a lot of the work is done through strategic storytelling.

And since I really can't tell if you're nodding yes to all of this right now, just to make sure you're sold on this whole "stories are awesome" bender I've been on, I'm going to give you one of the reports that goes along with that program as a bonus.

The product is $2,000. And you can't even get near it if you haven't already been working with me for awhile.

But because I want you to start getting use out of high-level storytelling right away, this extra report is all yours, free of charge.

I call it "The Hollywood Method of Engaging Your Audience." It gives you a behind-the-scenes insider look at a trick that top movie producers use to draw viewers in from the very first minute of a film.

And you can use this exact same tactic in YOUR sales and marketing.

So if you haven't done so already, head over to
www.ItDoesntMatterBook.com,
where you can get your hands on it, along with every other
bonus.  You greedy fucking muffin top, you.

Oh, and once you've got a hold of that, turn the page to dive
into one of the most important topics you'll ever be exposed to.
It's time to show you what it REALLY means to make someone
an offer they can't refuse...

# IT DOESN'T MATTER WHAT YOU'RE SELLING

# Move 4: Unleash the Power of an Irresistible Offer

Okay, pop quiz. How do you take whatever it is that you're selling ...and make it absolutely irresistible?

Easy.

In the words of Don Vito Corleone, you "make them an offer they can't refuse."

Yep, that's it. You make them an offer. A strong, irresistible, drop-dead sexy, shit-your-pants awesome kind of offer. One that'll have 'em more twitchy than the neighborhood heroin addict if they pass it up.

Now I realize that when I tell people how important it is to have a solid offer, sometimes they don't know what I mean exactly. So let's break it down a little more and really give you a solid picture here. This is a key point that will end up making you a lot of money when you get it right.

An offer is a more robust version of whatever product or service you're selling. It can be a collection of features, benefits, or promises in general. But at its highest and most effective level, it's actually a collection of more "products."

And that's the difference.

Amateurs sell stand-alone products or services.
Pros sell offers.

Now as you're reading this, it's possible your mind is already going to that place where you're worried because you assume your situation is different. You think all you have is a stand-alone product or service, and you really don't know how to make an offer out of it.

Well, this is why we covered positioning before anything else in the book. It's all about perceived value. And I don't mean to say that you need to just start making shit up. What I mean is that it's likely that you're already offering way more than you even realize. More than you're allowing your consumer to perceive.

But even if you don't already have a few extra things that have been hiding under your nose the whole time, you need to understand that you're more than capable of adding things to your offer that you had never considered before.

And once you figure out what it is that you can add, you simply need to figure out the best way to position it into your sales message.

Consider the iPhone, for example. Just a product, right?

Nope.

An iPhone may seem like a stand-alone product, but it's been positioned as an offer since day one.

In fact, go to YouTube and see for yourself -- when Steve Jobs first introduced it, it was at a press conference where he kicked things off by announcing THREE "revolutionary products":

"A widescreen iPod with touch controls."
"A revolutionary mobile phone."
and
"A breakthrough internet communicator."

It was only after lining these up frame by frame on his presentation slides that it was clear they weren't separate devices. They were all one product. But really, with the way they were described, they were actually all one OFFER.

And even outside the scope of that first press conference, the iPhone is still an 'offer' in many other ways today.

Apple has positioned your decision to buy an iPhone as a way for you to get:

- The "latest" phone technology
- The "best" camera on a phone (the truth is there are way better cameras on other phones, but most people will never learn this)
- The world's biggest collection of apps
- Perks of staying in Apple's ecosystem (free iMessage texts, Facetime, iTunes, and synching with other Apple devices)
- iOS and all of its features, including constant free updates
- A more secure/virus-proof operating system
- And more

This also works in reverse.

When Instagram was first developed, the photo part was just one small section of a larger app.

But that part was so impressive to the right investors (and the other parts were so unimpressive) that Instagram went with it and made it the central product itself. Then they built around it with private messaging, filters and more to make it an offer all over again.

You should have aspects of your product or service that are SO good that they could be their own 'product' to build around. And once they're that good, they can either actually be their own product for real OR they can be positioned to make what you're selling a way better 'offer.'

If you still think this doesn't apply to you, let's look at a few more examples:

Plumbers' offers should include peace of mind (both in reliability of their work AND availability in emergency situations).

A doctor's offer should clearly include access to the most advanced medicine on the market (even though we all know a lot of that is just a big scam -- but that's something for me to piss and moan about another day).

Facebook's "offer" includes easy access to long-lost friends, the ability to network for your job or business, the ability to advertise for your job or business, a sense of community, a sense of connection, a distraction from loneliness, convenience, entertainment, and invasion of your privacy (just kidding about that last one. Well, not really).

Facebook doesn't directly communicate all of these, by the way, but their functionality does a lot of the work for them since it's so addictive.

Google "offers" reliable, accurate, and relevant search results. But it also offers productivity and life tools for 'free' in G-Suite (I'm writing this book using Google Docs). And as of this writing, Gmail has 1.4 billion users. Take a look at all the features in Gmail alone and tell me that isn't an offer.

Think about those late night infomercials where the say "Buy 1, get 2 free. And you'll also get X product as a bonus that you can keep as a thank you for trying us out (even if you return the product)."

Remember, if you need to, you can put these kinds of perks into your sales messaging through the stories you tell. That's why we covered stories before going into offers. By this point, you can probably really see everything coming together on this. Every key move helps you with every other key move.

Let's take this even deeper. Getting back to the iPhone example, I recently saw a Russell Brunson video where he took a $500 iPhone and made a valid offer to sell it to you for $10,000.

Why was the price so high? Because it was HIS iPhone. With all of his personal contacts (including phone and email), his own personal business notes, AND information product recordings he spent over $500,000 on (that one alone makes $10K feel really small all of a sudden, doesn't it).

Imagine you were looking for investors and someone was selling a phone with Richard Branson's personal number. Or Bill Gates. Or another high-roller.

Imagine you were the world's biggest sports fan, and someone had the real phone numbers for Michael Jordan, Tom Brady, and LeBron James.

For the right person in the right industry, that's basically what was in Russell's phone. And if that's not enough to get you to pull out your wallet and buy it, keep in mind - there's only ONE of these. Once Russell sells it to one person, it's gone. And built-in scarcity always helps you raise that price.

So really, making a proper irresistible offer is about selling something to someone at a price that makes it an absolute no-brainer.

If you offer someone a Bentley for only $5000, no strings attached, they will find a way to come up with that money. Bring the price down to $700, and they won't let you out of their sight until the transaction is complete.

In other words, the more perceived value you're offering, the less expensive it feels.

How important is this? So important that people have reached out to me for the sole purpose of helping them create AND sequence their offer. And they've walked away very happy because they knew the key to making REAL money was in positioning yourself and your offer properly.

And if you still think you can't do this, I've got two things to say to you:

1- You suck. I fucking hate you. Okay, not really, but I wanted to get your attention because…

2- Here are even MORE examples to drive this home for you and help your brain start churning out a few ideas for what you can do:

Selling a spatula? Include a PDF or printed booklet of healthy pancake recipes. Maybe set up affiliate links through Amazon and point customers toward specific organic syrups or cookbooks (or something else related that will make the customer happier AND line your pockets a little more).

Working as a chiropractor? Don't offer Groupons like everyone else. Instead, have an offer that includes a spinal adjustment, deep tissue massage, nutrition consultation, energy healing book, weight loss plan, and list of vitamin supplements. Charge a few hundred dollars for this -- just like with the Bentley or Russell's iPhone, everything is relative. The price will be worth it to them.

Last example -- courtesy of Mr. Russell Brunson one more time (by the way, if you haven't heard of him before, one of the bonuses I have for you will show you how to get his most popular book for FREE. Just to be clear, we don't work together or even know each other yet. But I like his style and a lot of what he teaches, and it's an awesome book, so don't say I never did anything for you.).

What I learned from Russell is that you can often "stack" whatever thing you're already offering with other 'things' that fall into any of the following categories:

- Written Word (this could be a book, a pdf, a blog post, an article, or anything else you might read)
- Spoken Word (this could be a video of something, an audio recording, etc.)
- Physical Products (t-shirts, mugs, keychains, an extra of whatever you're selling, etc.)
- "Other" stuff (this could be a one-on-one consultation session, a meet-and-greet, access to a private Facebook group, or other "experience" for the buyer)

According to Russell:
"People will spend MORE money for the SAME product if it's packaged in a DIFFERENT way."

A great example he used is a DVD copy of "The Greatest Showman."

Based on the life of P.T. Barnum, a pioneer in business, the movie followed Barnum from early life all the way through his formative years where he became one of the world's most successful show business promoters.

Now the DVD itself sells for $20, but Russell wants to sell it for $100 instead.

So how does he pull that off? He does it with what I like to call a "value pile." Russell's word for it is stack, because what you're doing is stacking product on top of product as you build out your irresistible offer.

First, he offers the actual dvd itself.

Then Russell adds a book Barnum wrote about money, titled "The Art of Money Getting."

On top of that is another book about wealth by Barnum: "The Humbugs of the World."

Then, in addition to those physical print copies, he piles on a PDF copy of another Barnum book: Dollars and Sense, Vol. 1 and 2. These are old books, and getting your hands on them can be difficult and expensive.

But they're in the public domain, and Russell found a source for a high quality ebook that will be easy to read and enjoy.

After that, Russell finds Joe Vitale, who wrote a book about Barnum's philosophy of making money titled, "There's a Customer Born Every Minute," and he licenses the rights and convinces Vitale to allow the book to be included in this offer.

While he's at it, Russell records an audio interview with Vitale, who's a success in his own right.

The whole interview is centered around making money as an entrepreneur with very little start-up capital.

Then he piles on another PDF report by Vitale on Barnum's "Ten Rings of Power on Creating Fame, Fortune, and a Business Empire Today."

And if that's not enough, Russell stacks on access to a private Facebook group, just for business owners who want to take Barnum's ideas and apply them toward financial success.

Finally, Russell offers to have a group phone call where he shares his own thoughts on Barnum's philosophy and how anyone can use them to make more money.

Russell will share the recording of the call with everyone who ordered, even if they can't attend the call live when it happens.

Keep in mind that Russell has sold over $100 Million worth of his own products and services, so anyone who knows about him is going to want to hear what he thinks!

And now, after stacking all of those perks onto the value pile ...NOW we have ourselves a sexy offer that will be irresistible to the RIGHT customer (which we'll talk about more in the 'Market' chapter).

Now we've got something where people will pay $100 where they were previously only willing to spend $20.

If you take a close look at this offer, by the way, you'll notice it's based around the theme of making money...

## THE MOST MONEY CAN BE FOUND IN 3 'CORE' MARKETS

This is a key thing to keep in mind. Because while it's not 100% essential, IF AT ALL POSSIBLE, you're going to want your offer to fall into one of the three core categories of Wealth, Health, or Relationships.

Based on human psychology, this makes a huge difference in having a stronger and more appealing offer.

For example, a plumber can place an ad that shows a husband and wife no longer fighting over the leaky faucet (Relationships). Or an ad where their water is finally clean now that the pipes have been replaced (Health). Or how they saved X dollars thanks to the plumber preventing the basement from flooding (Wealth).

So you can probably see that if you really understand what your product or service has for the marketplace, this isn't as hard as you might think.

And make no mistake -- a great offer -- structured the right way -- and at the right time -- will make you rich.

If you want to try your hand at this and get your mind in the mode of coming up with some good offers for whatever you're selling, Russell recommends the following exercise:

Find something random in your own home and structure an irresistible offer around it.

It can be anything.

A DVD like Russell used.

An old computer.

Or even a book.

For example, I've got tons of marketing books on my shelf.

It would be very easy for me to pick any one of them and offer a deal that includes:

- Personal coaching calls with me on every chapter.
- Strategy videos where I implement some of the best advice in the book.
- PDFs of how I can apply tactics from the book in 5-10 different industries or markets.
- AND -- if I can swing it -- maybe an interview with the book's author. I can sweeten the deal for him by allowing him to make his own special offer during our talk (that can bring in more cash flow for his business). It's a can't miss for him since I'll be the one doing the hard work of marketing the interview. All he has to do is chat with me for an hour, sit back, and let the new customers roll in to whatever website he has me mention.

Part of this thought experiment should be your best attempt at piling on as much value as possible. Because you really want to push yourself to come up with something that has a super high price tag. So really ask yourself -- How high can you make it? Can you get your offer to $100. Awesome. Go for $1000 then. And $5000 after that. Really push the limits of your imagination. It will pay off in ways you can't even begin to imagine once you dive back into your own business and work on crafting your own new offers.

## THIS IS HOW YOU SEPARATE YOURSELF FROM THE COMPETITION ...AND RAISE YOUR PRICES WHILE YOU'RE DOING IT

In case it isn't clear yet, the whole point of this chapter is that you want to decommoditize yourself and whatever you're selling. And you do this by replacing whatever your product or service is ...with a robust and sexy offer.

And while most people don't realize it until they actually try it, if you do this right, you'll be able to outshine your competition and sell more than them, all while having way higher price points. We're conditioned to try and compete with others on price in hopes that this will make the difference for us. But it's a sucker's bet, and it's not sustainable.

So don't lower your price. Add more value instead. Because playing the 'cheapest on the market' game will usually make it very difficult to have margins that really serve you.

And if you can't be the absolute lowest price in the game, there is absolutely no competitive or strategic advantage to being the second lowest. So you might as well go the other way and position yourself as a more expensive (and more valuable) option instead.

When I work with people on adding more value into what they already have, they're often shocked at how easy it really is to position their company or their product so well.

I always enjoy either being there in person, or at least working with them through video conferencing, because the looks on some of their faces are priceless.

Nobody has allowed me to share any yet, but I have a few screenshots of recorded Skype call screens where you can literally see the clouds parting for the first time for some people, and they have the goofiest grins you will ever see on a human being. Think back to the movie 'Office Space' where Drew wants to give his next date his 'Oh face'. It's a little like that.

## IF YOU DON'T CREATE SOLID OFFERS, YOUR BANK ACCOUNT WILL HATE YOU

If you're still wondering if I create offers in my own business, please close this book right now and slap yourself across the face with it. If you're on a device like a Kindle or a phone, hit yourself with that. If you're on a classic old-school computer screen, please take that big-ass monitor, and smash it over your head.

YES, of course I create offers. That's my entire business model. I can't think of ANYthing I sell that isn't an offer. Even this book is an offer. Look at all the bonuses I've been including. Don't think for a second that I don't mention those when I'm telling people about this book.

And since it's so vital to do everything in your power to make sure your offer is irresistible to your audience, I've decided to make this chapter's bonus a summary report of a training I did on my own personal top 4 favorite elements of a perfect offer.

The original training was priced at $500. But it's no longer available to the public. So without this book, neither is this report. As with all the others, you can grab this bonus at www.ItDoesntMatterBook.com.

And you'll need it, too, if you really want to make the most out of our next topic: The Blueprint for Selling to the Right Market.

Turn that page, read that content, and get that ass of yours ready to make some bank. It's time to put yourself in front of REAL buyers…

# Move 5: Find the Blueprint for Selling to the Right Market

What is the one absolutely vital question you need to answer in order to figure out if you're going to make money in your market?

I'll tell you before this chapter is over.

For reals.

But first - story time. Not too long ago, an associate of mine was working on an information product that offered a VERY interesting solution in the weight loss industry. I can't go into specifics because as of this writing, he's looking into some patent stuff and might take this in a whole different direction. But for the purposes of this story, it doesn't matter what was specifically being offered.

What DOES matter is that the sales and marketing game plan he had created to go with the product was not only brilliant, but it was absolutely PERFECT for what he was offering. If you ask me, it was as close to a guaranteed sale as you could ever ask for in that market segment. He had it all worked out.

Now here's the key part to all of this -- He designed a campaign specifically geared around the way Facebook's mobile user experience functioned.

So in order for the promotion to be successful, everything he was doing needed to be done through Facebook itself. Otherwise, there would be no point to it.

So he went straight to work.

He spent nearly six months (and tens of thousands of dollars) putting together a ton of media assets, and organized everything else he was going to need in order to coordinate the campaign as seamlessly as possible.

I'd never seen him this excited before.

Think about it -- Imagine coming up with a product that you thought was finally going to bring you the millions you'd been wishing for all your life.

Imagine you knew exactly how to sell it.

Imagine your strategy seemed 100% foolproof, and all you had to do was execute it.

This was what it seemed like with this guy, and he went all in with no hesitation.

Experts were hired.
Ads were created.
Videos were produced.

# IT DOESN'T MATTER WHAT YOU'RE SELLING

Everything was ready to go.

And then as soon as he launches the very first ad, he phones me up freaking out about how Facebook flagged the content and told him he was violating their terms of use.

Not exactly his best moment.

Neither of us could figure out what he actually did wrong, but he couldn't get a straight answer from Facebook about what the issue was because every time he emailed them to figure things out, they sent back a canned response that didn't give him anything useful to go off of.

I'd been through a similar experience myself on a totally different product in another market segment. For me, it was particularly frustrating because every single email I got back was an almost identical reply, which was very weird and VERY confusing.

It's as if the recipient wasn't even reading my explanation and just copying and pasting a standard reply.

I originally thought it was staff outside the U.S. who just didn't speak English and kept sending cookie-cutter responses since they couldn't read what I wrote anyway.

But after telling this story to someone recently, I actually found out that it was Facebook's AI. Imagine that.

Rather than employ actual humans, they were using artificial intelligence to send canned replies and screw me over on my ad spend.

And here I was worried about the Terminator coming to life and running amuck out on the streets. But he didn't have any guns after all. Nope - that fucker had a "ban ad account" button on his screen instead.

Anyway, whether it was my friend's campaign going to waste, me getting cookie-cutter replies to my own emails, or anything else, this story is unfortunately way more common than you might think.

And by now you're probably wondering where I'm going with all this? What's my point? My point is this...

Before you go through the effort of building a product, opening a store, inventing a platinum tampon, or taking that sales position, you need to ask yourself something very important about the market:

## ARE THEY BUYING?

Seriously, are they buyers? Have you asked yourself this question?

Have you asked yourself:

- If you're marketing to people who WANT what you're selling?
- If you're marketing to people who CAN AFFORD what you're selling?
- If you're calling or emailing the DECISION MAKER?
- And (what my friend should have found out with a test campaign LONG before wasting months of his life on the marketing) ...if you're on a platform that will actually reach your audience??

Because if you don't answer these questions (and answer them honestly), you're in for a real long haul.

I'll never forget that hopeless look of disappointment on my friend's face. I'll never forget that tone in his voice as he went over everything, trying out what he did wrong, whether he could fix things, and how he could salvage all that time and money he poured into getting everything ready.

Pay close attention here.

Don't let this kind of thing happen to you.

Do whatever you need to do ahead of time to make sure that you're going to be in front of the right kind of buyers BEFORE putting in the wrench time.

In other words...

Do the work and make sure you're in a market of buyers. Buyers you have access to. With a message that speaks to them. With a product or service that will actually serve them. Ideally already buying from your competition and proving that there's really demand for what you've got.

There are people who get referred to me for JUST this part of the business. Because there are tricks to this. Little counterintuitive methods of making sure that people are actually going to buy what you're selling. This is the difference between 3 figures and 7 figures.

And until you've honestly answered the question of whether you're in front of real buyers, you're going nowhere fast.

Now if you want to go and invent something and change the world, be my guest. But I should tell you that as a general business rule, amateurs sell untested ideas. Pros, on the other hand, find out what's already selling and they make money off of that.

They find a way to differentiate themselves, of course. But they still choose to sell what people are already buying. Because the best indication that you're in the right place is that people are already pulling out their wallets for your competition.

Without that key indicator, your road to success will be messier than a grandpa's diapers after a field trip to Taco Bell. A Level-10 shit storm. Trust me.

# REMEMBER THE 3 CORES
# ...AND FOCUS ON ONLY 1

This is probably a good time to remind you of what I said in the last chapter about the 3 core markets of Wealth, Health, and Relationships. Even if your product or offer doesn't naturally fit into one of them, it's a very good idea to try and fit your SALES MESSAGE into one of them if you can.

When you focus on fitting them into one of the three cores (like I did with the plumber example), you'll have better attention grabs, more powerful stories, and sexier offers.

There's a lot more flexibility here than you might realize, by the way.

Soap can be marketed around health (hygiene in germ-filled environments) OR relationships ("smell like a real man, and she can't resist you").

Weight Loss can be health (a fit body for a long-lasting life), relationships (sex-appeal), and even money (stats proving that attractive people get more promotions and earn higher salaries).

Even Real Estate can dive into more than one. Wealth by flipping houses. Health by "peace of mind in a good neighborhood." Relationship by "getting the home you've always wanted together."

There's always a way once you get used to looking through the lens of a potential buyer and figuring out where they'll be most motivated.

But with that said, you need to stick to one specific angle out of the three. Conversions plummet every time they try to fit your sales message into more than one core angle. In fact, conversions plummet every time you try to sell with more than one idea altogether.

So even if your product will make someone rich AND help their love life, pick only one of those in your messaging. Because a lot of the people you're marketing to will already have one of those areas solved ...or they'll be too indifferent to solve both of them.

But when you target that one idea or motivation, you'll intimately connect your message to the right people who are highly-motivated to do something about it (like, say, pull out their wallets and spend money on you).

But taking this even further, if your product teaches guys how to have better body language around women AND how to talk to them (BOTH being in the same market of 'relationships'), you still only want to focus your marketing around ONE of those. Otherwise you risk diluting your message. And then your prospects don't trust that you can do either of those things.

# THE RIGHT PRODUCT
# FOR THE RIGHT MARKET

Now regardless of how well you're able to fit what you're selling into one of those 3 cores, rest assured that there are always strategies to position your product very powerfully.

But it still needs to make sense. In the end, you still need to have the right product for the right market. After all, it's just not in Apple's best interests to build an entire campaign around selling MacBook Pros to farmers. And it's not very helpful for tractor companies to try and sell to New York City residents.

So be sure that everything you're doing makes sense, and that you can clearly express a logical reason why what you're selling is a good fit for the people who are buying.

## HOW THIS ALL FITS TOGETHER

You might have noticed by now that this book is technically out of order. If I was going to map it out like a textbook, the actual chapter order would be:

Market (Chapter 5)
Product (Chapter 6)
Position (Chapter 1)
Attention Grab (Chapter 2)
Story (Chapter 3)
Offer (Chapter 4)

Notice how I put market before product -- because I care more about having buyers than about having something to sell. Without buyers, the product or service is pointless. Never forget that.

And if you're wondering why I chose to cover the market and product toward the end, it's because most people ignore them. They want the sizzle of all the other tactical stuff first.

I figure let me at least give you some high level strategy first so that when I dove into these final chapters, you'd understand the psychology behind everything better.

On top of that, when you actually understand the mechanics of the other topics covered in this book so far, you actually make way more intelligent decisions about your market and your product or service.

That's why these chapters probably seem to be getting a little shorter as we get to the end of the book -- you now have a more advanced level of understanding into all of this, so there's much less to explain. You're now ready to take things to the next level.

But first we have one more vital topic to cover: the product or service itself.

Remember, all your customer wants is to have their problem solved. And if you can't actually do that, it's career suicide to claim otherwise. But what if you have the reverse problem? What if you can do WAY more for them than you claim, and you don't even realize it? That's what we'll be diving into next.

But before we do, I've got another bonus for you.

I want to give you an example of how I fit a story around one of the 3 core markets (I chose 'wealth' in this case), and how I target it around a prospect like you who would be interested in learning more about sales and marketing.

The name of this bonus is: "How To Save $1,000 By Getting One of the World's Top Marketing Resources for Free." You'll understand why I call it that after you see the video that goes with it.

I'm technically breaking my own rule for you by pointing you to another information resource (outside of the bonuses that tie directly to this book's content), but I don't feel too bad about it because:

1- A LOT of what's represented in this resource is very much in line with what I've been teaching you.
And
2- The link I'll be giving you will allow you to get this external resource for FREE. You just pay a low shipping fee.

This is probably a good time to officially confirm that this is the first and only time in this book that I'll be giving you a link that ISN'T mine. So again, just to be 100% clear, the resource I'm pointing you to in this bonus is someone else entirely.

Anyway, this is alongside all of the other bonuses I've already shared. So you can get it by going to www.ItDoesntMatterBook.com.

Okay, time for another awesome chapter. Get ready to make some money off a product or service you can truly be proud of...

# Move 6: Make Your Product or Service Worth The Price

What if you could:

1- Be completely unapologetic and shameless in promoting what you sell

2- Mind-hack your prospect into spending money on you

And

3- Sleep well at night

...ALL by knowing you actually served them well AND provided real value for what they paid for?

I ask because not only is this possible -- it's actually HOW your customer wins.

This is the highest level of the game. This is how you stay congruent in your positioning -- even when you frame yourself as the best thing to happen to this planet since sliced bread. Or Batman.

This is how you craft the strongest attention grabs, tell the most powerful stories, and create the most irresistible offers.

It's also how you make sure you put your best foot forward in your market, no matter what the competition is doing.

How do you do it?

Easy - you sell a product or service that's worth more than what you're charging. That's it. That's all you need to do.

What, were you expecting some magical answer that wouldn't be that simple? I've got news for you -- the need for some magic bullet is the exact reason why so many people fail. But it's also the reason you're about to start making more money than you ever have in your life.

It's as simple as this -- If someone pays you a dollar and you're giving them something worth more than that dollar, you're doing them a service.

Same goes if they're paying you $10,000. Or $500,000. Or $1 Million. The figure never matters as long as you surpass it in value. Because it's not just about giving them something worth more than what they are paying for. It's about giving them something worth more TO THEM than what they are paying for.

So if some guy's got a full healthy head of hair, and I charge him $1 for a hair replacement product worth $1,000, I haven't actually served him. Because even though I gave him more in value than what he paid, it's not specifically useful to him.

But if he knows this and is choosing to buy anyway because he's planning on giving it to someone else as a gift or something, all of a sudden we're back in business.

Notice how it's the CUSTOMER who is choosing whether to buy it or not. And it's also the customer who's deciding whether it's worth the price.

So as long as you're being clear and accurate in how you sell something -- and as long as you're not intentionally trying to deceive them -- it's THEIR responsibility to make a good decision or a bad one when it's time to pull their wallet out.

And as long as you've got something that's truly worth selling, all you've got to worry about is demonstrating that quality to them.

So don't undervalue yourself. And just have a kickass product or service. And then, knowing full well that you're offering genuine value, go all out in selling it to anyone who needs it and will actually listen.

Now if you're wondering if it really is that simple after all, the answer is yes. And no.

You see, there are still two possible problems we've got here...

Potential Problem 1: You might be marketing or selling a product for someone else (as a salesperson they hired) that you don't think is really that good.

If that's the case, either find legitimate reasons that what you're selling is actually useful (ask your boss or your colleagues why they think it's a great product) ...or find a job selling something else as fast as you can. Because the sooner you believe in what you're selling, the better you'll perform when it counts. And that's when the money rolls in faster than Superman on a coke bender.

Potential Problem 2: You're already behind what you're selling, so you can already use what's in this book very effectively. But you wish you could make it even better. Or maybe it's already better, but you don't even realize it.

This is a slightly more complicated problem. But the people who solve it for themselves when they're making five figures -- they'll jump to six. Six figure stars will jump to seven. Seven will jump to eight, and so on. In other words, solve this problem for yourself, and you'll basically be adding another zero to your paycheck.

A key part of this that you really need to understand is that -- regardless of what you're selling -- it doesn't matter how (or if) it's valuable to YOU -- it's only about how valuable it is to THE CUSTOMER.

And depending on whether this is a physical product you're selling ...or a service you personally provide, the ways of establishing more value are a bit different...

If you're selling some kind of physical product, it all comes down to having a better awareness of its value so you can better communicate the real benefit to the prospect. One of the best ways to do this is to ask yourself questions like:

- "What does my product do that's really great? Better than anything else in my industry?"
- "Can what my product does be used to really help my ideal customer?"
- "HOW can what my product does be used to help my ideal customer?"
- "Based on what my product does well, who is my ideal customer?"
- "In what way does my product add convenience to the life of the customer?"
- "What problem for my customer is my product really solving here?"

You're basically doing a deep dive into what this can really be for the right consumer, and you're branding your product way more powerfully.

You're almost finding your product's "superpower."

But how do we guarantee that same level value when you're selling yourself? Simple. We do it by making YOU more valuable. We do it by finding YOUR superpower.
And this will require an upgrade to your mindset...

# UPGRADE YOUR OUTLOOK, REINVENT YOUR APPROACH, AND MAKE YOUR SUPERPOWER THE ANSWER TO THEIR PRAYERS

You know the old expression "it's not bragging if you can back it up?"

Well, it's time for you to be downright arrogant about who you really are and what you do. Because backing up that level of ego will challenge you to serve your customer in a way you never would have previously imagined.

How far do you want to take this level of arrogance? SO far that you literally consider yourself the answer to their prayers. Because if you look closely enough at whatever problem they're having -- you may very well be.

People literally pray to have their problems solved. So be the person that helps them better with these problems than anyone else out there. Have the superpower that they need you for. It's your church now. So answer that prayer of theirs, and make sure they put something good in the collection plate.

# IT DOESN'T MATTER WHAT YOU'RE SELLING

Take it from someone who already knows. I literally help people figure this out for themselves. And the results are usually pretty epic.

When I work with clients, we often reinvent their positioning in the span of only one or two calls. So it's obviously a really fast process for them.

But even though we don't take too long on it, what we end up with is often such a radical departure from what they've been doing, that they sometimes barely recognize themselves.

Because before we worked to show them what they TRULY have to offer, they just didn't have the confidence in themselves (or their product) to really position it in a way where the prospect is literally COMPELLED to buy from them.

It can be a bit of a shock to the system to see this power in action.

And once you see yourself from this new perspective, you can never go back. But you'll never want to either.

Okay, let's take some steps right now to help get you there... First thing, regarding your mindset in all of this...

Regardless of whether you're selling physical products, software, your own personal services, or anything else...

Regardless of whether this means showing someone how to use the product or doing it for them...

Regardless of whether you can easily see it in yourself ...or whether it's been hiding under your nose this whole time...

...You need to acknowledge the very real possibility that there's something special about you or your product that you can use to truly help that customer.

You can use it to help them understand WHY what you're selling is so valuable to them.

Or you can use it to help them figure out HOW to get the most value out of what you sell.

Or you can you use it to simply do an awesome and exceptional job for them.

And when you really get this, it helps you define and express the unique selling proposition of either you or whatever you're selling with killer precision.

Because the biggest hurdle here is that most people responsible for sales or marketing are often blind to their own brilliance.

So while you might be able to get this right away, you might also need to really think about it or even ask people around you who you trust.

It's easier than you think once you start to ask yourself the right questions.

So if you're selling yourself or a specific service you provide, you'll want to ask yourself questions like:

- "What do I do that's really great?  Better than anyone else in my industry?"
- "Can what I do be used to really help my ideal customer?"
- "HOW can what I do be used to help my ideal customer?"
- "Based on what I do well, who is my ideal customer?"
- "Where does my talent add convenience to the life of the customer?"
- "What problem for my customer am I really solving here?"

Answering questions like these for myself really gave me SO much more clarity when I was first starting out.

## MY SUPERPOWERS

Want a real world example of what can come out of this?  Well, let's look at me.

My superpower is that I see the hidden speed bumps in other people's sales and marketing approach. That's the short version, at least.

But to be more specific, some of the highest-value things I do for them include...

- Spotting choke points in their sales funnels.
- Identifying key segments of the market that they're failing to sell to.
- Revamping their sales messaging.
- Re-writing their copy.
- Adding curiosity gaps to their ads.
- Showing them how to raise their status in their industry.
- Helping them establish themselves as experts in their field.

I'd list more, but this is a book written for you, not a sales letter about me.

But since I want to teach you how deep this can go, I also want to add that sometimes people don't do as well as they should in their job or business because they just don't see the gaps between who they think they are ...and who they can really be.

That's why in addition to the tactical end of things where I give them solid strategies and techniques to deploy for their business, I also help people:

- Spot their own blind spots.
- See what's really possible in their product or service.
- Step up in their field.
- Obliterate Imposter Syndrome (this one is vital).
- Demolish doubt.
- Discover hidden gifts and talents that they can use to make more money.
- Speak authentically in their own voice to boost sales (authenticity NEVER fails).

But with all of that said, if I were to boil everything down to one specific superpower that I use in my own business, it would be:

Showing people where they're already capable of bringing in massive revenue for their business or employer -- and walking them through the steps of actually doing it.

A few important notes about my superpower list…

1- Notice I have more than one -- You'll obviously want to be able to condense your highest value to only a sentence or two when for when you need to do a fast pitch (like I just did above). But you should still ideally have more than one superpower in your arsenal, if possible. It makes your sales message and the actual value that you deliver more dynamic.

2- My awareness of these superpowers needs to be as deep as possible. Not only does it help that I realize what they actually are, but it's also extremely useful to understand WHY they're so special -- because that helps me use them even more effectively.

Ideally, your superpowers should be able to help others in some very clear and specific ways. And the only way to be sure that they're clear and specific is to be able to articulate (in either written or spoken word) how or why they are truly special.

For example, the reason my superpowers are so special is because they're geared toward helping others spot their own superpowers! I don't take this knowledge for granted, because it was NOT easy to come by. Which brings me to my next point...

3- If you think I figured out my superpowers 100% on my own, you're nuts.

Over the years, I have deliberately kept myself around people who were already on my level or way ahead of me in both life and business. And they've served as wonderful sounding boards whenever I needed feedback on my own progress.

After all, when I tell you that we don't see our own blind spots, I completely acknowledge that I've needed help with this in the past as well. To this day, I still bounce ideas off associates who are on my level or better. It's just good business.

Every time I help someone with a blind spot that they're struggling with is just another reminder that I never know if I still have a few creeping in the background on me. So I keep myself in check as often as I can.

I mention all of this because while you definitely want to figure as much of this out for yourself as possible, you also want to lean on others, if you can.

You can do it by asking for feedback from customers you've already served well. Or you can do it by checking in with people who are close to you and know you really well. Or find a mentor. Or hire someone to work with you on this. Or all of the above.

However you do it, though, you want to take this very seriously and make sure it gets done.

Failing to discover where you (or your product or service) truly serve others could literally be costing you millions of dollars a year.

With all of that said, there's one key thing here that often gets lost in the shuffle when all you're doing is spending the day thinking about why you're awesome...

## YOU STILL NEED TO KNOW IF YOU CAN HELP THEM BEFORE YOU SELL THEM

Make no mistake here. Despite all those superpowers I listed for myself (and the fact that it's only PART of my complete list), I still don't sell my time or services to just anyone. I've turned down many people who were not ready for me. I've turned people down who were not willing to take action. I've turned down people who had way too negative of an outlook on life to be successful. But most importantly, I've turned people down if I simply didn't think we'd be a good fit.

Because it isn't good business for me to just take anyone on, get a quick paycheck out of them, and then not be able to truly serve them.

My philosophy on this is very simple. When it comes to client satisfaction, ANY business relationship needs to be win-win.

From start to finish -- and beyond -- you've gotta be in your customer's corner in a way that nobody else has EVER been.

I believe this so deeply that I make sure my clients know up front that I expect a testimonial from them. Not want. EXPECT. The obvious catch here (in case it's not so obvious after all) is that I have to earn it. I have to MORE than earn it.

My attitude is that I want you so over-the-moon happy from our work together that you'll be racing straight to your laptop -- knocking over any old ladies and friendly pedestrians in your way -- to write a glowing review that makes me sound hotter than a latex thong in August.

That's the secret to over-delivering. That's why clients forgive me when I push them. Most importantly, that's how they listen long enough for me to sneak in and get them a holy shit result.

Take a pro tip from me and try it yourself for a week or two. You may surprise yourself. And hopefully your client while you're at it.

# THE SECRET SAUCE TO A PRODUCT OR SERVICE WORTH CHARGING FOR

That last thing I want to cover here is a reminder of why it's so important to sell something that has quality and offers genuine value. And it's true whether you're selling software, consulting services, coaching, skateboards, apple pie, tequila, condoms, dildos, or free weights (or all of the above - yuck - that's one party I won't be attending)...

Nobody buys because of the product. They buy because of the sales message behind it. And when they do that, they take you at your word that the product will actually deliver on every last promise your sales message made.

So work to make the most compelling sales message you can. And then simply make sure the product or service behind it always lives up to the hype.

That's the Secret Sauce. That's how you stay in business, scale your offerings, and cash those huge paychecks.

And on that note, I've got another book bonus for you. If you haven't gone to www.ItDoesntMatterBook.com yet for this or any of the other bonuses I've added, now is the time. The bonus for this chapter is called "How to Give Something Away for Free and Then Easily Charge More Money for Your Product Because of it."

This doesn't simply suggest you give something away for free. It tells you exactly WHAT to give away. It's a key counterintuitive psychological tactic that nobody ever thinks of (except for the people already making millions of dollars). Ignore this at your own peril.

It was part of a $100 product training I did. But it's yours for free right now. And you can thank me tomorrow.

But before you thank me, we've got one more special chapter to cover.

And if you think we aren't closing out this book in a big way, then you're nuttier than a squirrel's turd on Easter Sunday.

Pretend that reference actually made sense, and turn the page to our final chapter.

# Putting It All Together and Making The Moves

## HOW TO SCREW UP ANY CHANCE OF GETTING THE CUSTOMER TO BUY

A confused mind always says no.  And a prospect who isn't directly being spoken to never even looks.  So if you want to keep your revenue low and your stress levels high, go ahead and ignore the framework this book just handed you on a silver platter.

But if you're finally ready for something more, then follow the plan.

Position yourself with trust and authority.  Grab attention like a mogul grabs hoo-has.  Storytell like Spielberg on smack.  And make that offer sexier than a man who can make you laugh.

Wrap it all up in market-appropriate messaging to bring this bad boy home, cater it around the right product or service, and invite me to your yacht as soon as you buy it.  Because remember...

## THIS IS SIMPLE

Look, the goal here is simple:  Get them engaged, and then sell them something.

In the end, you're using nothing more than a message and an offer.  That's all it is.

Provide value. Get paid for it.

Once you really understand that, you can cut out all the extra nonsense you've been fed over the years and attack the finer points through the framework you just learned.

It really is that basic.
IT DOESN'T MATTER WHAT YOU'RE SELLING.

Take it from someone who successfully sold this book to you. It was no accident.

And once you really get this, all these extra little insights will emerge to help you enhance your process.

You'll buy ads on YouTube on the channel of someone you're competing with. And you'll pull their customers to you.

Then you'll realize you can do even better by targeting specific videos rather than the whole channel.

And you'll wear t-shirts that make fun of their slogans, which will diminish their positioning and strengthen yours. Or you'll come up with a way to reach consumers that doesn't even involve the competition.

There will always be more than one option. More than one way. More than enough money.

You'll figure out people who are stars in your industry, but not direct competitors. And you'll find ways to get their attention. Maybe you'll follow their podcast and be the first to review each episode as soon as it drops. Maybe you'll come up with strategies to improve their own business and send it to them without asking for anything in return. Maybe you'll fly yourself out to a trade show they'll be at, cozy up with people on their team, and network your way in from there.

Once you really get the hang of this all, you'll see that you can tell your stories anywhere. You can make offers that don't require money changing hands (like providing a high-value giveaway for someone else's audience and raising your own profile as a result).

The possibilities are endless. The road is at your feet. Move now and enjoy the success that follows.

## SO NOW WHAT?

Well, here we are. At that critical point at the end of every book where you either actually do something with what you just read ...or jump straight into your bag of Cheetos, fire up Netflix, and go through your childhood collection of nail clippings.

Yeah, I still think it's weird that you kept those, but I'm not even gonna judge -- as long as you actually do something with what you just learned in this book right now.

You may find yourself tempted to learn more after this, which is fine IF you're FIRST putting what I've just shown you into practice. You really want to start pulling in some bank ASAP ...because "trying shit out" is always a hell of a lot more fun when you've already got lots of extra cash lining your pockets.

So in addition to getting moving on what you just read, IF you really need to stay in "information-consumption" mode, my advice is to at least dive deeper into THESE specific topics, so that you can do them even more effectively. Make no mistake, what I've just revealed in these pages is the map to the treasure. Follow it, and success is virtually guaranteed.

If you focus even on small wins daily, you'll gain momentum, and that momentum will quickly lead to bigger and bigger wins. That's just how it works.

So at the very least, if nothing else, make sure you're making at least 2 or 3 little moves a day.

## SHOW SOME LOVE

Now if you really enjoyed the book and bonuses, by all means, please leave a nice fat review on Amazon.

I realize that I haven't exactly been gentle in the way I've communicated all of these ideas. It's definitely not lost on me that I can be a little too "extra" sometimes.

But I didn't want to give you some watered down message that wouldn't have helped you as much. So I just laid it all out there, warts and all.

Hoping you cracked a smile or two, but more importantly, that my foul language and questionable temperament kept you a little more engaged and helped you process the material way more comfortably. Remember - method to my madness.

So if you really got something out of this, I really would be grateful for a review so that others can be helped by this message as well. Let 'em know if I made you laugh, which would technically make me sexy according to the first page of this chapter. Sexy is always good.

Oh, and if you don't want things to end here, well then, join me and others like yourself as we navigate all those business challenges in front of us and win. Whether you're in marketing or sales or both. Whether you're the boss or you hate the boss. Whether you're beginner, intermediate, or advanced.

We're all always on our way up the ladder. And it's always better with friends. So be a part of our community. Check in on my Shatter The Mold Podcast. Or better yet...

# WORK WITH ME:

Anyone who used to listen to my very first podcast knows that I rewarded loyal listeners by offering them special consultation rates (that no one else got) as a thank you for helping the show grow in viewership and inspiring me to keep doing it.

I'd like to extend that same gratitude and reward my book's readers as well. So if you'd like to work with me on your sales or marketing needs, reach out to me through the bonus link I've provided throughout the book.

I can only assume my prices will always steadily increase, so I don't know what rates will be by the time you read this.

But I'll always cut some kind of favorable deal to those who reach out to me through here as a thank you for buying this book and, more importantly, taking action on your business or profession.

For your convenience, I added a contact form to the bonus site to make it easier for you to reach out to me and my team: www.ItDoesntMatterBook.com

I look forward to working with you.

Oh, one more thing. When I was sharing preview copies of this book, I had a bunch of people asking me...

So just to clarify, The Baller Method is still waiting-list only. It's my own personal playbook, so to speak, of getting my own sales for my business, along with results for my clients that they never thought possible. It used to be a special client-only perk for people who were with me for at least 6 months, but now it's a simple stand-alone product.

It'll be a least a couple hundred dollars to buy - maybe more by the time you read this. But the return on investment makes it an absolute steal. To apply to be on the waiting list for it, go to www.BallerMethod.com.

I wish I could tell you how long you might wait to get access to buy and enjoy the program, but I just don't know. It always depends on how many people I can take on and serve at that point.

It'll be worth the delay, but in the meantime, don't wait to have that in your hands before going full throttle with what I've already taught you.

And again, if you need immediate attention, you can still apply to be an actual client right now with no delay at www.ItDoesntMatterBook.com.

I'm putting this book out there at a time when I'm available to take on new clients personally if it's a good fit, but I don't know how long that will last. So by all means, feel free to reach out if there's interest, and with luck, we'll be able to work something out for you or your company.

But just so we're clear here, I don't work with tire kickers. You need to be taking action in your career or business already. You need to be highly-motivated. You need to move on strategies I give you without any hesitation. And you need to truly be willing to win.

## ONE LAST THANK YOU AND GIFT

With all that fun stuff out of the way, I just wanted to properly thank you for reading. I know I bonused you with something at the end of every other chapter, and I'd hate to break tradition now.

So in a blatant attempt to gain your favor enough that you might actually take a quick minute out of your day, post a fast review on Amazon, and briefly share your thoughts about all the value I stuffed into this book ...here's one more freebie for you.

"The 30-Second Pitch Script"

This is a special script that you can use in just about any industry, and for any product or service, to get your sales message out in a clear and engaging way.

In today's social media zero attention span culture, being able to get your entire pitch out in less than a minute is vital to your business.

If I look back on all the training materials I personally consumed to learn this for myself, the total bill for me came to at least $800.

But because you read ALL the way to the end of this book, I'm going to show you how I do it for free.

Like every other bonus I set up for you, you can get your hands on this one by going to www.ItDoesntMatterBook.com.

With that said, let's do a little math here. Just in case you haven't scored yourself any of those bonuses yet.

What I've given you here in this book can change everything in your business.

And I wanted to make sure you felt you got back AT LEAST 100x in value the money you spent on it.

But then I realized 100x wasn't enough for me.

My ego needs to know I did more.

So to recap, in addition to EVERYTHING you just learned in this book, all of your FREE bonuses will include:

- "The Ultimate Social Media One-Two Punch" ($200 Value)

- "3 Power Moves to Positioning Your Brand for a Quantum Leap." ($149 Value)

- "12 Killer Questions for Getting Into Your Prospect's Head, Understanding the Psychology of Why They Buy, and Creating the Very Best Attention Grabs." ($97 Value)

- "The Hollywood Method of Engaging Your Audience" ($2,000 Value)

- "4 Awesome Elements of a Perfect Offer." ($500 Value)

- "How To Save $1,000 By Getting One of the World's Top Marketing Resources for Free." ($20 Value)

- "How to Give Something Away for Free and Then Easily Charge More Money for Your Product Because of it." ($100 Value)

- "The 30-Second Pitch Script" ($800 Value)

That brings the value of ALL the bonuses that you're getting for FREE to a grand spanking total of $3,866.00!!!! All by simply going to www.ItDoesntMatterBook.com.

Oh, and by the way, if you look up at this list, it's another built-in bonus for you right here on this page! It's a solid example of a value pile. ;-) Along with the additional tip of adding a decimal point and the last two zeros to make me look like an even bigger deal.

You're welcome, enjoy, thank you for reading, and I'll talk to you soon.

-Andrew S. Kaplan (yes, the 'S' is for "Superstar")

48659426R00094